NAOMI LINDSTROM

MACEDONIO FERNANDEZ

SOCIETY OF SPANISH AND SPANISH-AMERICAN STUDIES

THE SOCIETY OF SPANISH AND SPANISH-AMERICAN STUDIES
PROMOTES BIBLIOGRAPHICAL, CRITICAL AND PEDAGOGICAL
RESEARCH IN SPANISH AND SPANISH-AMERICAN STUDIES BY
PUBLISHING WORKS OF PARTICULAR MERIT IN THESE AREAS.
ON OCCASION THE SOCIETY WILL ALSO PUBLISH CREATIVE
WORKS. SSSAS IS A NON-PROFIT EDUCATIONAL ORGANIZA-
TION SPONSORED BY THE UNIVERSITY OF NEBRASKA-
LINCOLN. IT IS LOCATED AT THE DEPARTMENT OF MODERN
LANGUAGES AND LITERATURES, THE UNIVERSITY OF
NEBRASKA-LINCOLN, OLDFATHER HALL, LINCOLN, NEBRASKA
68588, U.S.A.

Library of Congress Catalog Card Number: 80-53826

ISBN: 0-89295-018-8

SSSAS: LC-315

To David William Foster, mentor,
these volumes are gratefully inscribed.

CONTENTS

INTRODUCTION

I. A Writer of Lasting Originality

Only a few years ago, the idea of devoting a monographic study exclusively to the literary works and program of Macedonio Fernandez would have seemed capricious. When Macedonio died in 1952, at the age of seventy-six, he occupied a legendary place in the literary history of Buenos Aires. However, his legend had less to do with any substantive contribution to literature than with the author's extraliterary activities. Anecdotes circulated attesting to Macedonio's endlessly inventive conversation, eccentric manner of life, erratic writing habits and extreme reluctance to publish his work. To cite just one instance from the large corpus of Macedonio anecdotes, one acquaintance claims that the whimsical literatus first entranced him into a state of awe and then served him vinegar in a wineglass, correctly surmising that the substitution would go unnoticed.[1] Such entertaining but frivolous second-hand accounts formed, in large part, the basis for Macedonio's fame. This trivialized image, together with the fact that his works were so little read, did little to establish Macedonio as a force in Latin American literature. Literary historians felt justified in omitting any mention of such an eccentric or dismissing him, as Luis Harss does, as an «ingenioso conversador.»[2]

Yet even while Macedonio was more mythologized than read, certain voices insisted he was a genuine literary innovator, a propounder of significant literary principles and influence on the course of modern Argentine letters. Chief among these voices was that of Jorge Luis Borges, who proclaims himself the elder writer's disciple and heir: «Yo por aquellos años lo imité, hasta la transcipción, hasta el apasionado y devoto plagio. Yo sentía: Macedonio *es* la metafísica, *es* la literatura. Quienes lo precedieron pueden resplandecer en la historia, pero eran borradores de Macedonio, versiones imperfectas y previas. No imitar ese canon hubiera sido una negligencia increíble.»[3]

Borges was not the only one convinced of Macedonio's importance. Highly visible literary figures publicizd the obscure author's work, hoping to win for it a wider readership. **Raúl Scalabrini Ortiz,** for instance, includes Macedonio as one of the solutions to the national dilemma he discusses in his 1931 *El hombre que está solo y espera.* In a special section entitled simply «Macedonio,»[4] Scalabrini insists that every one of his readers ought also to become one of his hero's readers. His championing of Macedonio utilizes the most emphatic language. He states: «**El primer metafíscico de Buenos Aires y el único filósofo auténtico es Macedonio Fernández.**»[5] Although Scalabrini's work received enormous attention, few seem to have taken his injunction to read Macedonio. Despite such discouragement, Scalabrini maintained that his friend had much to say to great numbers of Argentines, not just to an élite. Throughout the late twenties and early thirties he continued to promote Macedonio's writings by word of mouth and in praise-filled published statements.[6] The poets Leopoldo Marechal and Oliverio Girondo also figure among Macedonio's vocal and enthusiastic supporters.

At this point, one may well ask why a writer with so much support and endorsement from within the literary community failed, until recently, to win any sizable readership. The first and most obvious answer to this question is that much of the Macedonian *oeuvre* did not find publication until the sixties and seventies. *Museo de la novela de la Eterna,* an attempt to re-invent the novel, did not appear until 1968, when Centro Editor de Buenos Aires brought out an edition. *Adriana Buenos Aires*, which advertises itself as «la última novela mala» in its subtitle, was not accessible until the 1974 Ediciones Corregidor version appeared. A number of the author's theoretical writings and prose pieces did not become public until very recently, and this effort of rediscovery will surely continue in years ahead.

Along with the discovery of unknown texts, there has been an enthusiastic republication of out-of-print ones. In 1961, Ediciones Culturales Argentinas brought out Borges's anthology of his mentor's writings. The 1966 Centro Editor edition of *Papeles de recienvenido* made a greater impact on the reading public. 1967 saw the same publisher's reprinting of *No toda es vigilia la de los ojos abiertos*. In subsequent years, Ediciones Corregidor became Macedonio's chief publisher. 1974 was the centennial of the author's birth and the commencement of the Corregidor line of complete works. This series, still quite incomplete, was to include both known works and miscellaneous writings found among the author's papers.

Macedonio's longstanding unread, unpublished status resulted from, among other things, his unusual mode of living the literary life. Emir Rodríguez Monegal concludes that Macedonio missed achieving major status because he lacked a «strategy.»[7] That is to say, he declined to engage in any promotional campaign designed to bring his work to the attention of the reading public. Nor did he attempt to gather disciples into a literary movement, as Rodríguez Monegal suggests he might have done. Macedonio' reforming zeal is evident in his writings, and he urged his friends to join in the creation of a new literature. Yet he made little attempt to proselytize anyone outside his immediate circle.

The most famous aspect of his deviant career was his lack of interest in seeing his own works into print. Marechal, Scalabrini Ortiz and others made the arrangements for publication. Even with such support, the author published only five volumes in his lifetime. The metaphysical *No toda es vigilia la de los ojos abiertos* was the author's first book, appearing in 1928 and followed by *Papeles de recienvenido* (1929), *Una novela que comienza* (1941), a short volume of verse, *Muerte es beldad* (1942) and an expansion of *Una novela que comienza* containing *Continuación de la nada* (1944). A posthumous book of poems appeared in Mexico in 1952, but much important prose remained unpublished.

This aberrant career was not only the result of neglect or diffidence. Macedonio abhorred the «official» literary life with its venerated authors and inanely passive public. *Papeles de recienvenido* features sardonic portraits of literary stuffiness with its attendant «recitado a la visita, las lágrimas periodísticas por el desalojo de una familia desamparada... los versos de los maestros al gran Sarmiento...»[8] The author who takes advantage of this literary climate to establish himself as a public figure receives special scorn: «En Biología con el Hombre aparece la conferenciabilidad vale decir, la boqui-abriencia audiente. Ninguna especie antes se dejó conferenciar...» (PR, p. 294). Macedonio wanted no part of this pomposity.

Failing to publish was one way of rebelling. Conceptualizing works and then failing to elaborate them on paper was also typical of Macedonio, by all accounts. Certainly, the ultimate deviation from accepted writerly comportment consists of not writing. What

Rodríguez Monegal describes as lack of any literary strategy thus becomes part of a larger literary strategy in which deviance, rupture and unwriterly behavior are key elements.

II. Macedonio as Precursor

Another possible explanation for Macedonio's limited contemporary readership is that he was too much ahead of his time, as are many drastic innovators. Readers who lacked the experience of similar works had nothing with which they could compare the inventive author's experimentation, and did not know how to respond to it. The demanding new works required them to use new skills that, as readers of more conventional work, they had not had occasion to develop. Consequently, the gap between what readers were accustomed to doing in the course of reading a novel and what Macedonio was asking them to do to read his novels was too great.

This explanation is especially interesting because, as it turned out, Macedonio's radical work prophesies so accurately the innovation that swept through the Latin-American fiction in the fifties and sixties, gaining world fame as the so-called «boom.» The very great resemblance between Macedonio's writings and literary program and those of the latter-day innovators has struck many commentators. The most interesting discussion of Macedonio's precursor role appears in Noé Jitrik's analysis of the novelistic reforms propounded in *Museo de la novela de la Eterna*. The literary principles the *Museo* expresses, both overtly and implicitly, amount to almost a guide to creating the *nueva narrativa* which emerged in the fifties and sixties. The great resemblance betwen Macedonio's poetics, formulated in the twenties and thirties, and that of latter-day writers also marks the innovator-reformer as an excellent prophet. As Jitrik points out, the novelistic reforms were to bear fruit at a future time. The reformer was speaking not of what he could accomplish in his moment, but of a «novela futura.» [9]

Future projects apart, what Macedonio actually wrote presents patent similarities to the achievements of «boom» year writers. The likeness is interesting because it might help explain the emergence of a new readership for the neglected, early works in the wake of the «boom.» Readers who have experienced *nueva narrativa* writings have developed readerly skills adequate to cope with a fair amount of disorientation, fragmentation, juxtaposition of disparate elements and a strong vein of irrationalism. Bringing these skills to the reading of Macedonio's writings, they have more of a notion how to reapond to the challenges and demands those writings present. In that sense, the *nueva narrativa* developed a new, hardier strain of readers willing to undertake the reading of such demanding works. As Scalabrini Ortiz points out, few contemporary readers were prepared to generate the effort required to make something meaningful out of a Macedonian text.[10]

Akin to the notion that Macedonio was too novel for readers to adjust to his demands is the idea that his innovation was perceived as threatening. According to this hypothesis, those who dominated the literary enterprise could not accept the reformer's challenges and hence ignored their far-reaching significance. As we shall see, one of Macedonio's main principles was that every aspect of literary activity ought to be continually re-examined to guard against fossilization, solemnity and rigidity. Needless to say, he was not presenting an easy or comfortable future for literature. Jitrik, for one, believes that Macedonio's commentary on literature and society was so disquieting that it often went unheard. In Jitrik's analysis, the contradictions inherent in trying to make literature meaningful in the context of a bourgeois society are evident in «el silencio que rodea obras como las de Macedonio Fernández.»

Jorge Lafforgue, too, asserts that Macedonio demanded more than contemporaries were willing to muster. According to Lafforgue, Macedonio failed to galvanize the literature of his day because «su radicalismo conceptual... y la dificultad de integrar sus propuestas... no podrían asimilarse sin deformaciones a la torpeza de una literatura muelle, aunque ya entonces sacudida en sus cimientos, entre otros pocos, por Macedonio Fernández.»[12] Borges concludes that contemporary admirers of Macedonio truly owed more to Leopoldo Lugones, whom they despised as an esthetic reactionary, than to a hero whose radical notions were beyond them.[13] Macedonio's demand that literature constantly reconsider its fundamental premises went unheard and unheeded. Alicia Borinsky can only find parallels to the innovator's concepts in the works of theorists writing some fifty years later.[14]

Given this situation, one is not surprised to find the *nueva narrativa* claiming Macedonio as an ancestor or kindred spirit. Julio Cortázar and Angela B. Dellepiane typify, respectively, the creators and the critics who have proclaimed the rediscovery of this

«escritor exhumado.»[15]   Jo Anne Engelbert has explored at considerable length the continuity between Macedonio's pioneering
work and the literary production of the 1960s and 1970s in Latin
America.[16]

III. Questions of Literary History

This study presents Macedonio's creative achievement. It cannot include any detailed consideration of his place within literary
history. In Chapter Three, Macedonio's irrationalist predecessors
receive some discussion. However, the reader should be aware that
the innovator's career gives rise to other important historical questions.

Investigators of these matters focus their efforts on four basic
problems: 1) specifying the relations between Macedonio and the
Spanish experimentalist Ramón Gómez de la Serna 2) clarifying the
Borges-Macedonio interinfluence 3) describing Macedonio's position with regard to the Buenos Aires vanguard of the twenties 4)
studying the rise of vanguardism within the context of *entreguerre*
Argentina.

Borinsky has studied the Macedonio-Ramón link using the
correspondence between the two. Housed in the Hillman Library at
the University of Pittsburgh, these letters touch on many topics, including metaphysics, nonscientific medicine, anarchism and
morality. Of most scholarly interest are those that develop esthetic
notions. In 1970 *Revista Iberoamericana* published a sampling of
the exchange on poetics along with Borinsky's
commentary.[17]   Subsequently, other letters became public in such
periodicals as *Hispamérica* and the now-defunct *Crisis* [Buenos
Aires]. In addition, Borinsky utilized them as material for her investigations into Macedonio's esthetic ideas.[18]

The correspondence began when Macedonio noted in the
Spaniard's writings a concept of literary creation close to his own
inclinations. He wrote the author, declaring himself a potential
writer «muy interesado en la Estética de la Novela.»[19]   Their exchange of thoughts continued as Macedonio became a writer,
Ramón went into exile in Buenos Aires and both men achieved the
status of cult figures on the vanguardistic scene.

Besides the correspondence, their friendship produced
elaborate whimsical public tributes from Macedonio to his mentor.

In one, he compares the reading of Ramonian texts to a «difícil y bella tertulia; (PR, p. 282)» on literary matters. Macedonio proclaims Ramón the first to reveal «la Versión a Delicadeza del cosmos estante y del acontecer conciencial» (PR, pp. 105-06). The reminiscences of contemporaries give further testimony about the eccentric disciple and mentor. Ramón and Macedonio had such minimal personal contact and claimed such a close spiritual bond that the Spaniard liked to claim him as a purely imaginary friend. [20]

Borges and Macedonio had a more complex relationship, because the influence between them was mutual. Rodríguez Monegal, Fernández Moreno and John Murchison have assessed this case of influence. Each concludes that Borges was not, as he gallantly claims, an unformed youth learning at the knees of an eccentric master. Rather, each man had special information and skills that especially suited the other's needs. Borges had first-hand knowledge of experimental tendencies in European literature. He helped the older man out of his artistic isolation. Macedonio fascinated Borges with his fantastic and novel ideas on all matters, ideas developed in relative solitude. Rodríguez Monegal states that when the two met, Borges already knew quite a good deal about stylish poetic creation. What he still needed, and what Macedonio provided, was «un Maestro y modelo de pureza poética.» [21]

Rodríguez Monegal notes that Borges was a selective disciple who ignored portions of his mentor's doctrines. For instance, Borges continued to work within the conventions of the «author» role, producing and publishing written works. [22] One might also observe that while Macedonio preached his favorite philosophical tenets, Borges used them for ironic effect. [23] Despite these large differences, Borge's work does reflect Macedonio's influence. Researchers have discovered a number of areas of congruence, principally in the two writers' metaphysical topics and verbal ludics. [24]

The Borges-Macedonio link produced a number of public salutes from one innovator to the other. Borges has written words of praise to attract readers to Macedonio's books; he delivered a eulogy at the elder author's funeral; he produced a special anthology of Macedonian writings. [25] Macedonio places tributes to Borges throughout his writings. However, these statements have more charm and whimsy than documentary value. For example, Macedonio states: «Nací porteño y en un año muy 1874. Todavía no, pero muy poco después empecé a ser citado por Jorge Luis

Borges con tan poca timidez de encomios que por el terrible riesgo a que se expuso con esta vehemencia comencé a ser yo el autor de lo mejor que él había producido.»[26]

Less of a case can be made for any profound influence between Macedonio and the young writers who lionized him during the twenties. Indeed, several commentators stress the superficiality of these relations.[27] These young enthusiasts of experimental art drew Macedonio into the activities surrounding the publication of the newspaper *Martín Fierro*. Although they received his eccentric public speeches appreciatively and published his written efforts, the youthful vanguardists seem not to have grasped the larger implications of his innovation. Chapter Three of this study gives some consideration to Macedonio's involvement with the group. The curious reader will find a large amount of documentation elsewhere on *Martín Fierro* and the movement of which the magazine is now emblematic.[28] Certain works that Macedonio contributed to the magazine appear in *Papeles de recienvenido* and provide glimpses of his life among the somewhat overexcitable *martinfierristas*. For instance, he warns Ramón about the endlessly festive group: «No se irá usted sin haber arriesgado su vida en todos los comedores de Buenos Aires» (PR, p. 105).

Complex, indeed, is the task of accounting for the great rise of vanguardism in *entreguerre* Buenos Aires. Critics have used various approaches to characterizing and contextualizing the period. Guillermo de Torre represents the effort to link Argentine vanguardism to the great European, and especially French, «isms» of 1910-30.[29] Another line of inquiry examines the evolution of an expressionist esthetic out of elements already present in Argentine, Latin-American or Hispanic literature. Allen W. Phillips, for instance, views twenties and thirties innovation as the revitalization and continuation of an exhausted Modernist esthetic.[30] Borges, in recent years, has also expressed his belief in such a continuum.[31] The relations of such literary «elders» as Leopoldo Lugones and Ricardo Güiraldes with the youthful vanguardists continue to be the subject of investigation for what they may reveal about this question of innovation versus tradition.[32] The general tendency of recent inquiry has been to undercut the vanguardists' claim to have virtually re-invented art.

Newer criticism also finds vanguardists among *entreguerre* writers who avoided the label. Such radical innovators as Roberto Arlt and Armando Discépolo were grouped with the «proletarian» authors of the so-called *Boedo* faction. *Boedo* writers emphasized the social function of art and reproached the *Florida* group, i.e., the self-professed exponents of vanguardism with an elitist concern for esthetics. The *Boedo/Florida* distinction, however, does not stand up very well under investigation. Several writers belonged to both groups and, despite their differences, the factions socialized together.[33] By de-emphasizing this dichotomy, critics have gained a wider perspective on the entire phenomenon of Buenos Aires vanguardism.[34]

Research has done much to elucidate the connections between creative persons, but the relation of vanguardism to contemporary society remains largely unexplored. Committed critics have sometimes directed their sociologically-based inquiries at vanguardism, but too often for purely denunciatory reasons.[35] More recent studies by Jitrik suggest the possibility of developing a less value-laden methodology for examining the massive change that took place in Latin-American literature during the 1920-40 period.[36]

IV.   Literary Practice as Implicit Literary Theory

This study must also leave aside the «philosophical» value of Macedonio's work. This is not to say that the ideas in his writings hold no interest. The author considered himself first and foremost a man of metaphysical concepts. His utilization of literary rhetoric to express these notions was a means to an end. Despite the frolicsome and sometimes nonsensical way he presents his key beliefs, Macedonio affirms their essential validity: «No tengo ninguna duda de la conocibilidad perfecta del Ser ni de la eternidad de la existencia y auto-reconocimiento de cada uno de nosotros» (NTV,p. 8). An outgrowth of his philosophy was a theory of social organization. Through a paradoxically «mystical» reading of Herbert Spencer, he evolved an anarchism predicated on fostering an intuitive understanding between all citizens. In one of his self-justifications, Macedonio posits his two great goals as the propagation of his metaphysics and the preaching of «la beldad civil, o sea la Libertad, el Estado Mínimo» (p. 55).

Contemporaries   took   Macedonio's   metaphysics   as philosophical writing of a serious order, as the discussion in Chapter Three of this study shows. *No toda es vigilia*, with its heavy emphasis on theoretical consideration of the ultimate questions, was the author's biggest success. At first, this contemporary attitude seems hard to reconcile with the tepid reception of the same writings half a century later. Jitrik and Germán L. García both state that Macedonio misperceived his true vocation; García sees this error as a sign of the author's generally distorted concept of self.[37] Dardo Cúneo suggests that Macedonio possessed the elements of a valid system of social thought but ruined them with a massive infusion of pseudomysticism.[38]

The key to this contradiction would seem to be that Macedonio's contemporaries held him to the standards of intuitive philosophy, a category no longer valid. The characterization of vanguardistic irrationalism in Chapter Three shows how convinced Macedonio's friends were that intuition could solve all problems. Macedonio's «philosophical» admirers seem not to care whether he could construct a plausible argument or perform logical operations. Rather, they attribute to him the irrational insights of a vatic seer. Borges says, «Entendía todo. Tenía la verdad de todas las cosas,»[39] Nor did Macedonio care to acquire the skills of the rigorous reasoner. Indeed, he was forever defending metaphysics against «las solemnidades de la ciencia» (NTV, p. 8).

Here the critic faces a problem. Large portions of the Macedonian *oeuvre* consist partly or wholly of statements on metaphysics, esthetics and social theory. Besides *No toda es vigilia*, one now has access to the previously-unpublished *Teorías* Corregidor included in its line of complete works. Philosophical assertions occur throughout the author's literary works as well; *Adriana Buenos Aires* contains long digressions on art, theory of medicine, sexuality and other topics. How should critics best treat these often obscure and oracular pronouncements?

Nélida Salvador represents a straightforwardly ideological approach. Her discussion of Macedonio's poetry and prose identifies key concepts in the author's creative work.[40] Salvador's search for ideas ultimately leads to a devaluation of Macedonio's work, which she finds to have too large a philosophical component.[41] Less extreme is the procedure of Fernández Moreno. The latter critic reports on Macedonio's concepts in a special chapter. Fernández Moreno refrains from evaluating the importance of Macedonio's philosophical theories, though he points out the enthusiasm they once generated.[42] Borinsky utilizes the innovator's overt pronouncements in her attempts to determine his poetic ideals, as does Engelbert.[43]

Jitrik, on the other hand, rejects this procedure. To his mind, the critic who uses Macedonio's stated ideas creates grave problems for himself. Because of the whimsical and disorderly presentation of these notions, the critic may schematize them and, in so doing, distort them. If he conserves their disorder, he may well turn his critical discussion into a replica of the «maraña macedoniana.»

The solution, Jitrik maintains, is to remove the critical scrutiny from «el nivel de las ideas.»[14] The best guide to what Macedonio envisions for literature cannot come from his overt statements. One must also look at the way in which he went about constructing his works, at his structural and linguistic innovations. Jitrik's method is to refer to Macedonian pronouncements on art only if they correspond to the author's creative practices. He emphasizes the formulaic, expressionistically distorted nature of the Macedonian text. The writing embodies the author's ideas, but in covert, devious ways.

The present study does not attempt to map out in detail Macedonio's idiosyncratic metaphysics. It surveys Jitrik's analysis of the *Museo* and applies his approach--the search for implicit esthetic principles--to works Jitrik has not examined: *Papeles de recienvenido, Adriana Buenos Aires* and *No toda es vigilia*, which exhibits certain features of a literary work. In addition, the third and fourth chapters examine specific passages from Macedonian texts, in an effort to provide the close textual analysis the author's work has not yet received. These approaches exclude from consideration Macedonio's purely theoretical-essayistic writings, but by so delimiting the study, I hope to be able to make a genuinely literary analysis and cover new critical ground.

V. Macedonio's Right to Self-Contradiction

A continuation of this problem of «Macedonian tangle» is the author's frequent violation of his own stated principles. In some cases, one may suspect the principle in question of being less than eternal dogma. For example, Macedonio boasts: «Nunca he usado personaje loco en novela... el loco en novela hace cuerda a toda la obra» (PR, p. 292). Borinsky notes the proscription on madmen as one of the concepts enunciated in the *Museo*.[15] However, a madman is an important character in *Adriana Buenos Aires;* various deranged persons figure in *Papeles de recienvenido*. It seems likely that the rule against madmen is essentially a rhetorical device to emphasize Macedonio's contention that literature must destroy belief in «objective» reality. Banning the madman, whose faulty grasp of reality is a function of his alienation, would be one move toward this goal.

More complex is the persistent affirmation of a poetic principle juxtaposed with the equally persistent violation of it. Such is the case with the author's objection to didacticism. For Macedonio's reader, accustomed to his continual talk of reforming literature, it is startling to read: «No he hecho arte explicado, es decir, poema o chiste o sonata con aclaración de las intenciones y recursos puestos» (PR, pp. 291-92). It is abundantly evident how censorious Macedonio is of any writer guilty of «instructividad.» He takes Francisco de Quevedo to task for this vice, though admiring the poet's humor. The use of literature to convey information about real-world conditions also appalls Macedonio (PR, p. 292).

The contradiction between the author's antididactic stance and his own didacticism is so patent that Macedonio exploits it as a humorous topic. After the quasi-autobiographical narrator of *Adriana* lectures the reader on the evils of scientific medicine, one finds this jeering footnote: «Esto es más que novelón; es hasta doctor» (AB, p. 191). While chiding Kant for his dogmatism and for forcing his arguments upon the reader, Macedonio discovers that he has been engaging in remarkably similar behavior himself (NTV, p. 153).

Two explanations may help reconcile Macedonian theory and practice. Firstly, the author is not claiming to write the «good» literature he espouses. He points out that the rhetoric adequate to his demanding poetics is not yet extant. While authors and writers still cling to outmoded patterns, they have begun to foresee an art free of «parentescos» and «subjetividad faltante» (PR, p. 283). Jitrik makes it clear that Macedonio offers a hypothesis of what the new writing might be, not a working model.[16]

Macedonio's role is to help mankind realize the literary future. As guide, he must preach the necessity of change to his readers. His own works must alternate exhortation with a tentative implementation of the new esthetic. Future authors will find all this work accomplished before they set out to write. Unburdened with the task of reform, they will be able to write «sin contexto» (PR, p. 138). Their rhetoric will be fully equal to their artistic designs.

Moreover, the inclusion of grave contradictions is a natural outgrowth of Macedonio's disorder. One of his chief tenets is the productivity of chaos, as in «La perfecta descompostura» (PR, p. 166). A disheveled narrative or a disjointed exposition of theory could provoke the reader into formulating his own insights. Any author who offers readers perfected elaboration deprives them of the irritating irregularities that give literature an interesting texture. Macedonio's cheerful disobedience toward his own precepts is another rupture with «todas las solemnidades escritas, habladas, versificadas, desde miles de años» (PR, p. 113).

One of the author's contradictions is disturbing enough to necessitate an advance warning to readers. «Bad» literature is one of Macedonio's key concepts, but this category can change quite drastically in what it includes.

One's first temptation is to equate Macedonio's category with a more recognized critical classification: the bourgeois novel, the conventions of «realist» fiction or the nineteenth-century positivist conception of literature. Many of the innovator's statements suggest such a congruence. *Adriana Buenos Aires*, for instance, claims to be a paradigmatically «bad» novel because of these features: «lenguaje hinchado» (AB, p. 58), «casualidades milagrosas» (p. 185), «profundidades y sutilezas psicológicas» (p. 213) and «la frase grandilocuente y lacrimosa» (p. 213). His opposition to representation in art is key to his esthetic program.

Literary history also suggests that Macedonio should be condemning the «bourgeois» novel. A great deal of negative literary criticism in Latin America has dwelt on the inadequacies of the realist author as social commentator and as artist. A number of recent studies on Argentine literature point out the inadequacies inherent in the realist esthetic of Manuel Gálvez, Eugenio Cambaceres, Julián Martel, et. al. These same works praise authors whose work is more expressionist than representational: Roberto Arlt, Armando Discépolo, Macedonio himself.[17]

This solution is neat, but not sufficiently complex to cover Macedonio's puzzling and shifting category. The discussion of the author's poetics in Chapter Two demonstrates that even the most innovative existing literature falls short of his expectations. Truly «good» literature can only follow a massive reform of reading and writing that will make readers co-participants in the production of literary works. Thus Macedonio can praise Franz Kafka for being «good» relative to his time, but within the current scheme, all literature turns «bad.» The curious status of «good» writers in a «bad» system is one of the innovator's most-exploited paradoxes. These individuals struggle to give their best to a passive, demanding reading public, which withholds the collaborative effort that could make literature «good»: «Por eso nos lastima mucho pensar en el destino de los que fueron universalmente señalados en escribir bien...» (PR, p. 86). Macedonio generates much confusion by confounding his terms of «good» and «bad» literature with reference to these talented creators and their sluggish readership. Amid this disorder, one should heed Wolfgang Kayser's advice to critics of expressionist writings. Kayser reminds them that the chaos of such works is a manifestation of a particular esthetic and world-view.[48] Rather than submit the dishevelment to rational ordering, they should supply a positive interpretation that respects the work's own premises.

VI. Delimiting the Body of Macedonio's Writings

Because of the delimitations of this study, Macedonio's poetic production cannot merit consideration. The author wrote poetry simultaneously with his prose and conceptual work.

The poems appeared in Mexico the year after his death, funded by an admiring relative, Gabriel del Mazo. Several appear again within the text of the posthumous *Adriana Buenos Aires* and a selection is reprinted in *Papeles de recienvenido*. These poems are not as original or complex in their elaboration as the author's other works. What really places them outside Macedonio's main plan of innovation, though, is not their quality. Jitrik points out that Macedonio's verse fails to show how literature may change or renew itself in the future.[49] It is a verse turned toward the literary past, in particular, toward the model of Edgar Allen Poe. A critic might investigate the intertextual correspondence between Macedonio and Poe. However, the connection between the two writers becomes more complex and explicit in the *Museo*, when Macedonio «borrows» Poe's Lenore to use as a character in his own writing.[50] The use of literature to question literature itself, central to this study, is infrequent in Macedonio's poetry, but omnipresent in his prose.

The study of the author's work must also take into account the non-written «novels» he invented. Many of Macedonio's radical schemes bypass the written text altogether, taking him into the realm of what would now be considered conceptual art or process art. His desire to author the unwritten manifests itself in such schemes as the following: «Sí, entonces, cuando combinaba con Borges, Scalabrini, Dabove, una novela sin tapas, que se iba a ejecutar escena por escena en la calle. La única novela que no se podría prestar.» (AB, p. 232). Readers of the *Museo* receive a number of invitations to enter the work as full-fledged characters.

In a departure from previous criticism, I have chosen to consider Macedonio's nonwritten novels as potentially realizable works and therefore as part of his total *oeuvre*. Macedonio's numerous schemes for a fiction without paper and ink, often cited for their whimsical appeal, receive their first sustained critical consideration in Chapter Two. Such discussion is possible because of the existence of two types of written documentation. One is the variety of proposals for a «Novela Salida a la Calle (MNE, p. 21)» scattered throughout the creator's writings. The other is the testimony of friends and acquaintances with whom Macedonio fantasized about the realization of an unwritten literature. The fact that these reminiscences seem offered in a merely anecdotal spirit does not invalidate their contribution to understanding a difficult concept. Macedonio's real-life actions and his literary production are not altogether separable. It is part of his literary scheme that literary reform extends beyond texts and lectures into all areas of thought and behavior. Rodríguez Monegal observes: «su obra es inseparable del hombre, de su anécdota, de su leyenda.»[51] One might agree with this statement but emphasize that Macedonio, author of the unwritten, is not just an individual eccentric but a model of what authors will do in his envisioned future.

Above all, Macedonio's production should be seen as an imperfect implementation of his ideals. As a visionary, he did not expect to see his own schemes put into practice in his lifetime. Instead, he directed his efforts toward a coming era in which readers would be more inventive and autonomous.

This study seeks to make an original contribution through its presentation of Macedonio not only as a forerunner figure but as a radical innovator in his own right. Moreover, it is important to see Macedonio's work as quintessentially representative of this century's most important currents of drastic cultural change. The parallels between Macedonio and other radicals, both creators and such theorists as the French structuralists and poststructuralists, are extremely useful in exploring this representivity. In addition, it is important to continue Jitrik's search for the embodiment of esthetic principles to those Macedonian writings the Argentine critic does not consider. Finally, in the third and fourth chapters, there is an examination of specific passages in Macedonio's writings to show how his principles manifest themselves in the verbal texture of the work. I hope the reader will emerge with a picture of Macedonio as a literary inventor in line with his century's radical esthetic thought, yet able to stand on his own as a literary thinker and a creator of literary work.

NOTES

1. Fedrico G. Pedrido, cited in Germán L. García's book of interviews, *Jorge Luis Borges, Arturo Jauretche, et. al. hablan de Macedonio Fernández* (Buenos Aires: Carlos Pérez, 1969), p. 41

2. Luis Harss, cited in Jorge Lafforgue, «La nueva narrativa actual,» in his edition of *Nueva novela latinoamericana, 2* (Buenos Aires: Paidós, 1972), p. 17.

3. Jorge Luis Borges, cited in Lafforgue, p. 17.

4. Raúl Scalabrini Ortiz, *El hombre que está solo y espera* (Buenos Aires: Editorial Plus Ultra, 1964), p. 125.

5. Scalabrini, p. 125.

6. Scalabrini, «Macedonio Fernández: nuestro primer metafísico,» *Nosotros*, 23, 228 (1928), 235-40.

7. Emir Rodríguez Monegal, «Borges and Paz: Un diálogo de textos críticos,» *Revista Iberoamericana,* 89 (1974), 573.

8. Macedonio Fernández, *Papeles de recienvenido* (Buenos Aires: Centro Editor, 1966), p. 293. Further references to this edition will be designated PR with the page number following. The following designations will also be used: MNE for *Museo de la novela de la Eterna* (Buenos Aires: Corregidor, 1974), AB for *Adriana Buenos Aires* (Buenos Aires: Corregidor, 1974), NTV for *No toda es vigilia la de los ojos abiertos* (Buenos Aires: M. Gleizer, 1928).

9. Noé Jitrik, «La 'novela futura' de Macedonio Fernández,» in his *El fuego de la especie* (Buenos Aires: Siglo Veintiuno, 1971), pp. 151-88.

10. Scalabrini, *El hombre que está solo y espera,* p. 125.

11. Jitrik, «El escritor argentino: condena o salvación,» in his *Escritores argentinos: dependencia o libertad* (Buenos Aires: Editorial Candil, 1967), p. 14.

12. Lafforgue, p. 18.

13. Borges, *Leopoldo Lugones* (Buenos Aires: Editorial Pleamar, 1965), p. 80.

14. Alicia Borinsky, «Macedonio: su proyecto novelístico,» *Hispamérica*, 1, 1 (1972), 44, 47.

15. The citation is from Angela B. Dellepiane, «Diez años de novela argentina (Boom, best-sellers, premios),» *Problemas de literatura*, 1, 1 (1972), 60. See Julio Cortázar's remarks to Ernesto González Bermejo in the latter's *Cosas de escritores* (Montevideo: Marcha, 1971), p. 102.

16. Jo Anne Engelbert, *Macedonio Fernández and the Spanish American New Novel* (New York: New York University/Center for Inter-American Relations, 1977).

17. Borinsky, «Correspondencia de Macedonio Fernández a Gómez de la Serna,» *Revista Iberoamericana*, 36, 70 (1970), 101-23.

18. Borinsky, «Macedonio: su proyecto novelístico» and *Humorística, novelística y obra abierta en Macedonio Fernández*, Diss. University of Pittsburgh, 1971. Borinsky's work is superseded by Jitrik's «La 'novela futura' de Macedonio Fernández» and *La novela futura de Macedonio Fernández* (Caracas: Universidad Central de Venezuela, 1973). The Macedonio-Ramón link receives consideration in Naomi Lindstrom, *Literary Expressionism in Argentina: The Presentation of Incoherence* (Tempe, Arizona: Center for Latin American Studies, Arizona State Unviersity, 1977).

19. Fernández, letter to Gómez de la Serna, cited in Jitrik, «La 'novela futura' de Macedonio Fernández,» p. 151.

20. Pedrido, cited in García's interviews, p. 40.

21. Rodríguez Monegal, «Borges, Macedonio y el ultraísmo,» *Número (Montevideo), 4, 19 (1952), 177.*

22. *Ibid.* Fernández Moreno makes the same point, pp. 21-24 of his study. John Murchison observes that, unlike Borges, «Macedonio mistrusted literature as a valid or even worthy enterprise,» in «The Visible Work of Macedonio Fernández,» *Books Abroad*, 45, 3 (1971), 432. This essay, 427-34, is a discussion of the elder author's influence on Borges. It also appears in *The Cardinal Points of Borges,* Lowell Dunham and Ivar Ivask, eds. (Norman, Oklahoma: University of Oklahoma Press, 1971), pp. 55-62.

23. Borge's skepticism is most notably discussed in Carter Wheelock, *The Mythmaker: A Study of Motif and Symbol in the Short Stories of Jorge Luis Borges* (Austin: University of Texas, 1969).

24. See Marvin Staff, *Jorge Luis Borges* (Boston: Twayne, 1970), p. 19, 60, 61, 88: Borinsky, «Macedonio: su proyecto novelístico,» p. 44 and Leopoldo Marechal's remarks in García's interviews, p. 73.

25. Rodríguez Monegal lists Borges's tributes to Macedonio, above-cited article, pp. 175-76. The eulogy is quoted here and in García, p. 7, p. 34. Borges prepared and prefaced the 1961 Ediciones Culturales Argentinas anthology, *Macedonio Fernández*. See also Borges, «Macedonio Fernández,» *Sur* 209-10 (1952), 145-47.

26. Fernández, cited by Rodríguez Monegal, p. 178.

27. See especially Lafforgue, pp. 17-18 and Rodríguez Monegal, pp. 171-75.

28. See Beatriz Sarlo Sabajanes, *Martín Fierro (1924-1927), antología y prólogo* (Buenos Aires: Carlos Pérez, 1969), Eduardo González Lanuza, *Los martinfierristas* (Buenos Aires: Ediciones Culturales Argentinas, 1961), Cayetano Córdova Iturburu, *El movimiento martinfierrista* (Buenos Aires: Ediciones Olivetti, 1967) and his *La revolución martinfierrista* (Buenos Aires: Ediciones Culturales Argentinas, 1962), Nélida Salvador, *Revistas argentinas de vanguardia (1920-1930),* (Buenos Aires: Univ. de Bs. As., Facultad de Letras y Filosofía, 1962), Oliverio Girondo, *El periódico Martín Fierro* (Buenos Aires: Galerna, 1968). Borinsky summarizes Macedonio's involvement with vanguardist reviews in her «Correspondencia de Macedonio Fernández a Gómez de la Serna,» p. 101.

29. See, for instance, Guillermo de Torre, *Historia de las literaturas de vanguardia* (Madrid: Ediciones Guadarrama, 1965).

30. Allen W. Phillips has worked extensively on establishing the continuing process of innovation that led through the various stages of modernism into expressionism. In Phillips's analysis, the modernist esthetic was continually subject to drastic revisions which ultimately became another movement altogether. See, for example, Phillips's *Tema del modernismo hispánico y otros estudios* (Madrid: Gredos, 1974).

31. See Borge's above-cited book on Lugones, pp. 75-80, for his «revisionist» assessment of the older author's influence. As a member of the youthful vanguard, Borges had earlier shared in the group's repudiation of Lugones, but now feels himself indebted to this embattled individual. Borges takes the notion of a continuous tradition even farther in the preface to his volume of verse, *El oro de los tigres* (Bs.As.: Emecé, 1974), pp. 9-10.

32. See, for example, Peter R. Beardsall, «Güiraldes' Role in the Avant-Garde of Buenos Aires,» *Hispanic Review*, 42, 3 (1974), 293-309.

33. A point Marechal makes in his interview with García. Marechal says that the two groups were really «unidos» p. 74.

34. Jitrik challenges the validity of the dichotomy in «Bipolaridad en la historia de la literatura argentina,» an essay in his *Ensayos y estudios de literatura argentina* (Buenos Aires: Galerna, 1970), pp. 222-52. David Viñas makes a case for the expressionist tendencies of two *Boedo* writers in «El escritor vacilante: Arlt, Boedo y Discépolo,» in his *Literatura argentina y realidad política: De Sarmiento a Cortázar,* ed. rev. (Buenos Aires: Siglo Veinte, 1971), pp. 67-73. Prieto also de-emphasizes the differences between the two groups, pointing out the dual affiliation of several writers, in the preface to his *Antología de Boedo y Florida* (Córdoba, Argentina: Universidad Nacional de Córdoba, 1964), pp. 7-35. See also González Lanuza, «Florida versus Boedo,» in his above-cited work, pp. 100-03.

35. See, for instnace, Viñas, «El escritor vanguardista,» in his above-cited volume,

pp. 60-66.

36.   Jitrik works in this vein in *Ensayos y estudios de literatura argentina*. The reference to the social context is less prominent, but clearly a component, in his *El fuego de la especie* and even the highly structural *El no existente caballero: Ensayo sobre la idea de personaje y su evolución en la narrativa latinoamericana,* (Buenos Aires: Megápolis, 1975). In this respect, see also the socially-contextualized commentary of Juan Carlos Ghiano, for example, «Cronología de crisis,» in his *Testimonio de la novela argentina* (Buenos Aires: Leviatán, 1956), pp. 19-37.

37.   Jitrik, «La novela futura de Macedonio Fernández,» p. 154; García, *Macedonio Fernández: la novela en objeto* (Buenos Aires: Siglo Veintiuno, 1974), p. 12.

38.   Dardo Cúneo, *El romanticismo político* (Buenos Aires: Ediciones Transición, 1955), p. 88.

39.   Borges, cited in Rodríguez Monegal, p. 175.

40.   Salvador, «Macedonio Fernández y su poemática del pensar,» *Comentario* (Buenos Aires.), 11, 38 (1967), 45-54, for poetry; «La negación de la realidad en los cuentos de Macedonio Fernández,» *Comentario,* 14, 56 (1967) 9-18, for prose.

41.   Salvador, «Macedonio Fernández y su poemática del pensar,» p. 45.

42.   Fernández Moreno, p. 12.

43.   Borinsky purues this tactic in both her above-cited articles, Engelbert in her above-cited book. Engelbert also bases a summary of Macedonio's «Metaphysics» on the author's overt statements.

44.   Jitrik, «La 'novela futura' de Macedonio Fernández,» p. 154.

45.   Borinsky, «Macedonio: su proyecto novelístico,» p. 37.

46.   The very title of the above-cited work brings this point home.

47.   See the works of Jitrik and Viñas, cited above; also, David. W. Foster, *Currents in the Contemporary Argentine Novel* (Columbia, Missouri: University of Missouri Press, 1975).

48.   Wolfgang Kayser, *Interpretación y análisis de la obra literatura,* 4a. ed. rev. (Madrid: Gredos, 1961), pp. 192, 230.

49.   Jitrik, «Poesía argentina: aislamiento y esperanza,» in his *Escritores argentinos: dependencia o libertad,* p. 41.

50.   Jitrik discusses the implication of Macedonian «borrowing» as well as this entire aspect of deliberate intertextuality in «Entre el dinero y el ser: Lectura de *El juguete rabioso,* de Roberto Arlt,» *Dispositio,* 1, 2 (1976), 128.

51.   Rodríguez Monegal, p. 177.

THE REFORM OF READING
AND WRITING

I. The Need to Rethink Literature

Macedonio's contribution is above all that of an innovator, a creator determined that literature must not continue to be the way he finds it. Casting a fresh eye on the literature of his time, he sees everywhere the marks of conventionality, fossilization and stagnation. His discontent makes him attempt the reform of literature; he seeks to make it new and productive.

This pattern of revulsion and reform fits Macedonio's career so well that it becomes a topic for his hyperbolic humor. In the *Papeles de recienvenido,* the newcomer of the title is an alien to the literary world and hence able to see its conventions as arbitrary rather than necessary. His editors try to tell him that his writings must be «cercados o sea contenidos por un cerco y que tuvieran la solución cerca, y, además, que ocuparan un solo lugar.»[1]   The untainted newcomer cannot see the validity of even these basic literary presuppositions. Casting his new eyes on the literary scene, the newcomer experiences an exaggerated revulsion. In an extreme state of innovative rebellion, he complains that his editors would domesticate literature into a clerical task demanding only office skills. Even the laws of physics place unacceptable constraints on his freedom of expression.

Through such hyperbole, Macedonio conveys a genuine dissatisfaction with the current state of literary activity. For instance, he groups all novels yet written as a single genre, the bad novel, although some may be considered near-novels. *Museo de la novela de la Eterna* proclaims itself the means to creating the first good novel in human history. Like the angriest young vanguardist, Macedonio tells readers that the literature of the future will be a vast improvement over the sterile literature of today.

29

The reformer's zeal, though exaggerated for comic effect, is real. Thus one is surprised to find Macedonio praising the creators of past literature and his literary acquaintances. Macedonio's writings are full of praise for the individuals who have written this unsatisfactory literature: Cervantes, Ramón Gómez de la Serna, Marinetti and the many *entreguerre* figures toasted in the *Brindis de recienvenido* section of *Papeles de recienvenido*. Even more surprising, though, is Macedonio's praise for a number of Argentine writers who have contributed little to the creation of his envisioned new novel. He says Argentina should feel proud of having had «a Estanislao del Campo... a Hernández; a Sarmiento, Vélez Sarsfield, Wilde; Alberdi; a Mitre... a los dos Ameghino; Muñiz, los Ramos Mejía; a Juan B. Justo, economista-sociólogo eminente y prosista magistral» (PR, p. 58). One's initial reaction is to think that Macedonio has abandoned all criteria. The indiscriminate grouping of such disparate authors in a generally praiseworthy category seems far from the sweeping dismissal of all past literature as invalid.

Here one must remember Macedonio's staunch belief in what Gérard Genette calls «L'Utopie littéraire.»[1] That is, he sees the entire literary enterprise as drastically in need of reform. Within the present, deficient system, authors cannot succeed except in a very limited fashion. Society views literature as a finished, manufactured product to be absorbed by the consuming public. This attitude dooms even clever and talented writers to «nada genial» (PR, 58).

It is for this reason that Macedonio's more inflamed statements are not directed against writers for failing to write well, but rather against those who control the literary environment. Editors, prize-awarders, all those who run the literary establishment, become targets of the author's most abrasive irony. The newcomer in *Papeles de recienvenido* is continually engaged in some imbroglio with his stodgy editors. A secondary stream of mockery aims at the negative critic who is unhelpful to the authors of the world but «los espera, en su casa, con un ceño y una ronquera terribles, si vienen de escribir mal» (PR, p. 86). Only those who seek an alternative to the literary *status quo* escape this sarcasm.

Readers have not done a very proficient job of reading, but Macedonio does not blame them any more than he blames authors for the stagnation of literature. Rather, he sees them as victims of a widespread misconception. Brought up with a truncated, unipolar scheme of literature, readers can only imagine themselves as consumers of a finished work. When an innovative work tries to move them toward the other pole, that of literary invention, their initial response may be faulty. For instance, Macedonio describes in fanciful terms the reading public's attempts to deal with his new, demanding writings. Having grasped that standard reading habits are of no avail, «a veces sus lectores tenían un volumen en las manos y otro en la oreja; y encendían el uno con el otro» (PR, p. 26). Macedonio recognizes that readers will experience a difficult period of transition from passive reception to active co-creation. His outrage is not with the readers who cannot read more imaginatively, but with the sterile model of reading that limits their imaginations. It will take many years of such misfired attempts as the one described above to evolve «las refinadas conciencias artísticas de autores y oyentes de los humanos del futuro» (PR, p. 138). Macedonio's attitude toward readers is always one of encouragement and support. He expresses confidence in their ability to meet the challenges of a literary project «en la que se espera tanto del lector... de su originalidad» (PR, p. 26). The *Museo de la novela de la Eterna* features numerous sections full of friendly advice and encouragement to readers. Even the reader who persists in subjecting the work to a conventionally linear reading is offered the author's forgiveness and a chance to repent in a special «Imprecación para el lector seguido» (MNE, p. 130).

Both authors and readers, then, appear as well-meaning participants in a fundamentally misconceived literary undertaking. To reestablish literature on a more productive basis, Macedonio works both at an overt, theoretical level and through practical strategies built into the structure of his work. The more visible aspect of this plan is the open warning to readers and authors not to continue the error of their ways. These expressed doctrines constitute a first step in the reform of reading.

The great flaw in the conventional scheme of reading and writing, according to Macedonio, is its artificial division of labor between authors and readers. Authors must assume all the responsibility for creation, while readers are limited to a purely receptive role. This apportionment is a mistake, because it ignores the inventive capacities of the reader and the author's desire for an active response to his communication. Author and reader are «dos descontentos de los que estamos; yo escribiendo, usted leyendo y de buena gana nos intercambiaríamos» (PR, p. 117). This blocked situation prevents even brilliant authors and readers from achieving a satisfying literary transaction.

The Macedonian programmata on this point are of special importance because of their close relation to developments in literary theory that have shaped twentieth-century critical practices. Particularly salient are the resemblances between Macedonio's ideas and those of the Russian and Czech formalists, on the one hand, and the French structuralists and poststructuralists as well. This kinship demonstrates again the Argentine's ability to articulate concepts that were just on the verge of appearing on the intellectual scene. He is a prophet because of his comprehensive overview of the transformation of artistic theory and creation in our time.

Roland Barthes, for instance, has worked with many of the same notions as Macedonio. Like the Argentine, he is especially interested in the reader's behavior toward the literary text. Of special interest are those readers whose reading habits deviate significantly from the cover-to-cover reading endorsed by society. These eccentric readers deserve our attention because they may illustrate alternatives to the stagnation inherent in traditional passive reading.

> Rereading, an operation contrary to the commercial and ideological habits of our society, which would have us 'throw away' the story once it has been consumed ('devoured'), so that we can then move on to another story, buy another book, and which is tolerated only in certain marginal categories of readers (children, old people, and professors), rereading is here suggested at the outset, for it alone saves the text from repetition (those who fail to reread are obliged to read the same story everywhere), multiplies it in its variety and its plurality: rereading draws the text out of its internal chronology ('this happens *before* or *after* that') and recaptures a mythic time (without *before* or *after*);... Rereading is no longer consumption, but play (that play which is the return of the different).[2]

Barthes's ideal, like Macedonio's, is a reader who makes the work new and utterly his own by the most inventive and participatory mode of reading possible. Conversely, the ideal authorial conduct is one that allows the reader the maximum freedom to experiment and create:

> The goal of literary work (of literature as work) is to make the reader no longer a consumer, but a producer of the text. Our literature is characterized by the pitiless divorce which the literary institution maintains between the producer of the text and its user, between its owner and its customer, between its author and its reader. This reader is thereby plunged into a kind of idleness--he is intransitive; he is, in short, serious instead of functioning himself, instead of gaining access to the magic of the signifier, to the pleasure of writing, he is left with no more than the poor freedom either to accept or reject the text: reading is nothing more than a referendum. Opposite the writerly text, then, is its countervalue, its negative, reactive value: what can be read, but not written: the readerly. We call any readerly text a classic text. [3]

As is immediately apparent, Macedonio's complaint against previously existing literature, or, as he classified it, «bad» literature, is very like Barthes's discontent with the literature the latter calls readerly. The «good» literature the Argentine envisioned for the future is like Barthes's writerly literature in its liberation of the reader's inventive energies. Just as Macedonio denies any author the option of writing «good» literature, since the reader's participation is needed to make the author's work «good,» so Barthes states: «the writerly text is not a thing, we would have a hard time finding it in a bookstore.» [4]

The strong parallel between Macedonian and Barthian, or, more generally, structuralist theory will become more apparent when we examine the hedonistic view of literature as play. In relation to Macedonio's efforts to create the «good» novel and the «good» reader, other parallelisms are evident. The question of reader competence, of great importance in the creation of the first «good» novel, has received much study as an area of structuralist literary theory. Jonathan Culler's overview, *Structuralist Poetics*, for instance, devotes a chapter to considerations of reader competence. [5]

The term *reader competence* did not come into use, of course, until after Macedonio's death. It comes from Noam Chomsky's distinction between linguistic competence and linguistic performance, a distinction that has proved especially useful and fruitful. Reader competence is the accumulation of knowledge and skill that a reader carries around with him and can use when he confronts an actual written work. Functional literacy is a competence everyone is expected to have, but some readers develop more complex, esoteric capacities. They harbor the ability to make an interpretation, to recognize various metrical schemes, to penetrate the intimidating syntax of certain baroque works or to date and attribute a work on the basis of its stylistic traits. Literary work may place special demands on a reader's competence in a particular area. The reader of Rubén Darío's 1896 *Prosas profanas,* for instance, must be able to identify the numerous mythological figures alluded to therein and grasp the relation of the referent to the literary work.

Although the discussion of reader competence under that name postdates Macedonio, he has the same concern. He speaks of giving the reader an opportunity to exercise his «capacidad» (MNE, p. 262) and of maintaining the reading public «vivaz y curtido» (PR, p. 56). The skills Macedonio wants his readers to develop correspond to some extent with the traditional abilities of the very competent reader. The Macedonian reader should bring great portions of his erudition, life experience and reading experience to bear on the new text he is confronting. However, the Argentine expects other competencies going considerably beyond the traditional receptive skills. His readers must learn to exercise their «fantasía» (MNE, p. 262) and participate in the invention of literature. As we shall see, creative reading is also a skill that demands constant cultivation, just as do the traditional receptive-reader competencies. Macedonio is determined to create systems to train competently inventive readers, just as the educational system now trains readers to receive literary works capably.

Macedonio also makes use of a concept associated with the theories of the Russian and Czech formalists: that of deviance as the productive element in literature. In the Macedonian reform program, startling the reader is of utmost importance. To invite the reader to a «good» reading, the author must move him away from his ingrained «bad» literary habits. By confronting the reader with something deliberately «de mareo» (PR, p. 171), the author can shock him into abandoning his accustomed attitudes and behaviors. In this plan, disorientation receives a high literary value. Here is where Macedonio's teachings resemble those of the Russian and Czech formalists. For these theorists, «foregrounded» language has the greatest power of artistic expression precisely because of its startling deviance from the norm.

Bohuslav Havránek explains the distinction between what is

nonpoetic and what is poetic:

> By automatization we thus mean such a use of the
> devices of the language, in isolation or in combination
> with each other, as is usual for a certain expressive pur-
> pose, that is, such a use that the expression itself does
> not attract any attention, the communication occurs,
> and is received, as conventional in linguistic form and is
> to be 'understood' by virtue of the linguistic system
> without first being supplemented, in the concrete ut-
> terance, by additional understanding derived from the
> situation and the context...By foregrounding, on the
> other hand, we mean the use of the devices of the
> language in such a way that its use itself attracts atten-
> tion and is perceived as uncommon, as deprived of
> automatization, as deautomatized, such as a live poetic
> metaphor (as opposed to a lexicalized one, which is
> automatized).[6]

In this scheme, literary expression was by its very nature aberrant. Jan Mukárovsky categorically states that the more
foregrounded the language in a work is, the more that work constitutes literature.[7] The deviance jolts the reader out of his passive
consumer habits and engages him in the act of creation.

Macedonio sees merit not only in linguistic shock tactics, but
also in drastic structural abnormalities. *Don Quixote*, for instance,
represents a move toward the ideal of a disturbing literature,
throwing the reader into an altogether productive state of
metaphysical commotion. It does so by presenting the hero complaining that an inaccurate story of his life has been circulated. The
reader, faced with a character who also has a life story outside the
novel, experiences «mareo». The violation of the common-sense
notion that literary characters have no existence outside the work in
which they occur is worthwhile. The «dizzied» reader must rethink
the entire concept of literary character. Macedonio states that
readers of this passage suspect themselves of having a fictional
status, since a character with apparent liberty has an unsettling
resemblance to a real-world person. Confusing the reader is a step
in the right direction, because it moves the reader from uninvolved
absorption of someone else's text to active confrontation with the
most troubling issues literature can raise.

Over and over again Macedonio expounds the necessity of involving readers' imaginations and inventive capacities. The ideal reader practices «el entreleer que es lo que más fuerte impresión labra conforme a mi teoría de que los personajes y los sucesos sólo insinuados, hábilmente truncos, son los que más quedan en la memoria» (MNE, p. 129). To the highest category of art, the author would admit only those works requiring a very high degree of reader activity, even reader agitation. The most-quoted assertion of this principle is the definition of *Belarte*, the elusive poetic ideal. To qualify as *Belarte*, a work must elicit «la conmoción de la certeza del ser de la conciencia en un todo.»[8] A literary work making lesser demands on its readers is automatically a lesser art form. Whereas the old conception of art put the activities and thoughts of author and characters in the foreground, the new art would feature those of the reader.

However, as nearly every Macedonian pronouncement on esthetics is couched in playful, enigmatic language, the reader cannot grasp this new scheme of literature until he sees its implementation. Macedonio is the foremost practitioner of his own preachings. The «novela en que el lector tenga que pensarlo todo» while the author «está inmóvil» (MNE, p. 252) only exists in the mind of the utopian author and his shocked readers. Still a demanding novel «cuyo relato se hace a escondidas del lector» (MNE, p. 21) is a move toward a noble goal. Macedonio cannot write his ideal literature, but only illustrate the direction in which literature must proceed to reach the ideal. As the author points out, all of his works remain within the realm of «bad» literature until a deep-seated change in reading habits and in the general literature occurs.

Despite their provisional, tentative status, Macedonio's reader-involving strategies still tell us a great deal about his utopian scheme of literature. Let us look then at some of the structural devices meant to provoke the reader into abandoning his passive role.

II.   More Responsibility for the Reader

Macedonio's envisioned reformation of literature, as he outlines it, requires the reader's creative contribution. The problem, though, is that most readers lack the skills required to participate in such a venture. An oppressive literary environment has deprived them of the free exercise of their inventive faculties. They expect the author to present them with a completed text requiring no further elaboration on their part. The author who demands too original a reading is a disquieting alien, «aquella diferente persona notada en seguida por todos...llegado recién a un país de la clase de los diferentes...» (PR p. 36). When the innovator's expectations for what readers can contribute are too high, disastrous results may occur: «ocasionáronse desventajosas comparaciones con el papel en blanco y sobrevino la nostalgia de esta clase de papel, que debe haber existido alguna vez» (PR, p. 26). Clearly, readers cannot acquire an entire new set of reading competencies overnight. Their powers of literary production will have to develop gradually.

The most dramatic instance of Macedonio's gradualism is *Adriana Buenos Aires*. In the prologue to this work, the author promises to give the reading public one last bad novel before subjecting it to the rigors of the first good one, *Museo de la novela de la Eterna*. However, he reserves the right to deviate somewhat from the conventions of the bad novel. Readers are warned that the supposedly conventional love story contained therein lacks an ending: «Los buenos lectores de novela mala tendrán que perdonarme el no detonante desenlace» (AB, p. 14). As we will see, the last of the bad novels contains more deviant features than the prologue admits. Yet, on the whole, it represents the Macedonian strategy of leading the reader to the new novel by degrees, meanwhile cultivating his inventiveness.

A gradualist strategy especially common in Macedonio's view, skipping, is one of the few creative abilities in use among the reading public. Skipping is one way the reader can wrench control of the literary event from even a reactionary author, for, as Barthes observes, «the author cannot...choose to write what will not be read.»[9] Part of the responsibility for the final form the work takes lies with the skipping reader.

Macedonio wants skipping readers to view their habits in a positive light. Barthes, in much the same spirit, notes we only skip when «no one is watching» although it is one of the reading behaviors that affords the most control over and pleasure in the text. To grant skipping its due as a legitimate, productive model for reading, Macedonio proclaims himself, as well as everyone else, a skipper: «Está debidamente codificada entre todos los lectores del mundo la regla de ausentarse después de la cuarta línea; a esta altura yo, cuando leo, suspendo.» (PR, p. 40). Acknowledging this practice can be liberating for literature. The author's responsibility for the final elaboration of the text can be openly diminished and part of it turned over to the reader. The skipping reader will not be seen as reading wrongly, or delinquently, but rather, as Barthes says, «boldly.»[10] Skipping can become a recognized part of the literary mechanism; Barthes gives it such a status when he states: «it is the very rhythm of what is read and what is not read that creates the pleasures of the great narratives.»[11]

The virtues of skipping, then, become especially important to the writer who invites creative reader participation. Rather than grip his readers' attention, fearful lest they grow bored and omit some of his pages, he should foster reader skipping. The obvious way to force readers into skipping is to write work which will be unreadable by any conventional reading. Thus the author proclaims «Lo advertimos porque quizá la lectura no lo dé a ver; con la presente obra entendemos hacer el lanzamiento, la primera entrega, la soltura, despavorido lector, de la inesperada y acreditada Literatura Confusiva y Automatista, de lectura fácil (de omitir)...»[12] Those who persist in submitting this innovative work to an unimaginative, linear reading find that «Todos sus defectos se hicieron públicos así» (PR p. 26). However, readers who can devise new, more aggressive modes of reading will find these «defects» to be invitations to exercise one's own skill as a writer, reworking the disordered text into something good to read.

Skipping as a creative act is especially important in *Museo de la novela de la Eterna,* a work which unabashedly proclaims itself to be unreadable. Here skipping is placed within the context of the overall plan for a new literature. The author warns readers they will not find many of the features by which literary works announce that they are completed, responsibly authored, worth reading and, in short, literary.[13] Readers who expect their literature to show its kinship with other literary works and disassociate itself from less-than-literary works will have to readjust. Now they must make literature out of a work which appears to be the result of a remarkably slipshod editing and structuring. No matter how attentively they may read it, it is not sufficiently written to provide the substance for a satisfying and literary reading. The editing and structuring are the reader's job.

The author points out the superficial resemblance between his work and work which is merely inadequate or nonliterary. «No hay peor cosa que el frangollo, si no es la fácil perfección de la solemnidad. Este será un libro de eminente fracaso, es decir la máxima descortesía en que puede incurrirse con un lector, salvo otra descortesía mayor aún, tan usada: la del libro vacío y perfecto» (MNE, p. 14). Noncompliance with reader expectations is justifiable when those expectations are part of a sterile conception of literature. The innovator's task, Macedonio insists, is to liberate literature from this «empty, perfect» scheme, not to comply with its implied demands.

Thus Macedonio launches a novel whose productive «botchiness» will force readers to make their own modifications. The most notable feature of his purposeful imperfection is the barrage of prologues which takes up slightly more than half of the book. Besides their number, the prologues disconcert by their seemingly inane redundancy. Moreover, the main body of the novel fails to reassure the reader that the work is progressing. Although more and more pages go by, no plot emerges and the characters acquire none of the properties that literary characters are conventionally given by a «perfect» author. The result is a work which literally provokes its reader into skipping.

Macedonio welcomes this display of independence on the part of readers: «Al lector salteado me acojo» (MNE, p. 129). Indeed, he dedicates the novel to this reader (MNE, p. 129) and makes him an indispensible partner in the refurbishment of literature. The skipping reader is the only one who can keep himself sufficiently entertained to eventually finish all of the novel. Whereas readers attempting to read from beginning to end will quickly fall by the wayside, the skipping reader will exercise his inventive powers to an unprecedented degree.

Freedom to restructure and abridge literary work means that each new reader will generate a new version of it. Macedonio recognizes and accepts such democratization of the novel. His willingness to accept aberrant styles of reading extends even to the most extreme cases. One prologue proclaims it acceptable to peruse only book covers and titles: «el Lector de Tapa, Lector de Puerta-Lector Mínimo, o Lector-No-conseguido, tropezará por fin aquí con el autor que lo tuvo en cuenta...» (MNE, p. 83). According to convention, those who limit themselves to advertising blurbs and booksellers' displays are remiss. Yet Macedonio's playful description of this particular contingent of the reading public legitimizes their conduct as a secret form of defiance.

Of all possible approaches to a literary work, only one draws Macedonio's scorn: linear reading. Although it is officially held to be the right way to absorb literature, the page-by-page mode strikes Macedonio as utterly unimaginative. Whereas each skipper creates a fresh text, the doggedly linear individual adheres to a single, unalterable model. Macedonio scolds one such plodder as «el que arruinaría y delataría» (MNE, p. 130) all attempt at innovation.

In a prologue aimed at the page-by-page audience, the author urges them to abandon their page-by-page reading habits and enjoy the liberty of skipping within the text. He accuses them of an «orientación en el arte que practicas de ensartar un día tras otro llanamente de tu sólida cotidianidad que te hace cenar plácido cada noche pensando en el almuerzo del día siguiente...» (MNE, p. 130).[15] The qualities of this «good» reader are bourgeois virtues antithetical to artistic expression. Thoroughness, order and rationality are here opposed to «misteriosidad» (MNE, p. 130), a property only unusual readers can enjoy in the work.

Thus Macedonio makes literary behavior represent the reader's total approach to life. Those who reorder the work, read only odd bits or blurbs on dustjackets, in short, the rulebreakers, are his ideal readers. Their disregard for fossilized convention-makes them potential collaborators in an innovative artistic venture. Macedonio's fondness for these mavericks extends even to those who refuse to read at all. *Adriana Buenos Aires* is prefaced by an interchange between the author and a rebellious reader who balks at the work's subtitle, refusing to read any further. The author, recognizing this revolt as a manifestation of reader independence, answers the quarrelsome reader good-humoredly. As a final tribute to the importance of reader input, the contentious reader's complaints are placed at the head of a list of comments by the author's prominent literary friends. The reader's reaction is part of the literary work, and precedes the opinions of Borges, Scalabrini Ortiz and other literary lights.

III.   «Os dejo contaminados...»

The option not to read a work in the order in which one finds it is a minor form of reader freedom. Because of this option, every novel that is written allows a great many novels to occur. Each time an independent reader re-edits the work, another work comes out of it. However, skipping is still a low-grade form of creation. Macedonio's next strategy demands more of the reader's creative potential. Rather than merely reorder what already exists, the reader must invent new elements.

Again, Macedonio recognizes the reaction such a request may elicit from readers. Indoctrinated to respect the text «as the author intended,» modern readers feel hesitant to intrude their own creations into such sacrosanct territory. Their ingrained passive habits make them feel inadequate to the task of co-creation. They may simply be too idle to bother generating part of the work. The conviction the author should be sole creator and the only one responsible for the final elaboration dies hard. Macedonio parodies this attitude in the complaints of an outraged reader who accuses the author of shirking his duties: «Sí, fácil es ahorrar trama cuando se carece de imaginación; ¿cómo concluye tu novela? (MNE, p. 252). However, this disgruntled reader comes to accept the new concept of literature, and Macedonio clearly expects as much from real-life readers.

That fictionalized ordinary reader is objecting to a device common in Macedonian writings: the incompletely elaborated text. It seeks to move the reader toward free invention by degrees. The author does most of the elaboration of the text, but omits some feature of the work which he then instructs the reader to provide. An especially explicit use of this technique occurs near the end of the supposedly conventional novel *Adriana Buenos Aires:*

> Ahora queda al lector. Reine desde el siguiente renglón el lector.
> El lector dirá si en esta novela el personaje Estela debe o no ser presentado con ulteriores actividades de cortesana, o ser salvada por el Arte de ello, dándosela por logradora de un pleno éxito de gran amor en su primera salida.
> (La comida sin Estela de todos sus amigos; la inmensa curiosidad; lo que se conversó; la alegría de su éxito tan pronto; los temores de su error, y todo lo más, serán labor del ingenio del lector-autor). (AB, p. 252).[16]

While in the above passage the passing of responsibility to the reader is patent, in one form or another such a delegation of authorial duties occurs throughout Macedonio's writings. Most typical is the omission of any clear-cut ending. Since readers feel a special need for closure, they are naturally eager to bring the proceedings to an esthetically satisfying end. The author can take advantage of this ingrained human tendency by abstaining from writing the ending himself and leaving the task to readers already caught up in the work.

Papeles de recienvenido, a series of journalistic notes, leaves the reader in such an unsatisfied, productive state. The author's ceasing to write is not the ending, he tells the reader, but rather a handing-over of the matter to the reader: «Breves seremos: traemos más que escuchar, que de decir: un público de privilegio como vosotros debe hablarnos cuanto antes...» (PR, p. 52). The author insists that the crux of his note is not in what he writes on the page, but rather in the resonances it provokes in the reader. The author's role is to start the processes of reflection in the reader and withdraw before he intrudes, standing back «para oír cuanto antes la sugestión de vuestro vivir de inquietud» (PR, p. 52). Authoring becomes the labor of setting up a situation or problem full of productive possibilities, but refraining from pursuing any of those possibilities. As one troubling essay ends, «Os dejo contaminados con estos problemas de que adolezco» (PR, p. 59).

Macedonio's inconclusiveness also serves a second function: to make readers more aware of how a literary work obtains its effects. After all, many literary works leave the reader with puzzling questions, but few make their open-endedness patent. Macedonio draws attention to the open character of his writings by leaving them in a visibly truncated form. He points out what he is doing: «huyo de asistir al final de mis escritos, por lo que antes de ello los termino» (PR, p. 34). His seemingly amputated endings proclaim themselves an esthetic virtue. Over and over the reader receives reminders that he is being saved from a passive reading.

Texts without endings are the most patently incomplete of Macedonian writings. However, other elements of the work may also be the reader's responsibility. The basic strategy remains the same: the author sets up the possibilities and the reader explores them.

Adriana Buenos Aires contains among its prefaces a «Guía de omisiones» in which the author lists some elements he has left out of the published work. Typically, the guide is capricious, listing such nonessentials as the pens used to write the work. However, the mention of omissions is not frivolous at all. *Adriana Buenos Aires* really does contain a number of startling absences. The first is the absence of any real explanation for the subtitle: «última novela mala.» Here the author expresses an intention to finish once and for all with the fossilized conventions of literature by complying with them utterly. The work at hand will represent everything that is dying, and ought to die, in literary expression. But this intention does not correspond to what Macedonio actually does in the novel. *Adriana Buenos Aires* manifests many innovative features along with a sentimental love story. Moveover, it is unclear why the purposeful writing of a mawkish love story should prevent future writers from writing pointlessly mawkish love stories. Macedonio does not flee from the contradictions inherent in his announced project. Rather, he draws attention to them. In a page of «Autorizadas opiniones» (AB, p. 15), he cites a «reader,» Borges, Scalabrini Ortiz and other literary figures and a future author. The opinions of these individuals all express puzzlement, bemusement or incredulity at the author's proposal; the «reader» finds it so flimsy he nearly refuses to read the work. Evidently, *Adriana Buenos Aires* stands in some relation to genuinely cheap love stories and makes some comment on such writing. The reader must work out for himself what that relation and that commentary consist of. He cannot passively accept the author's statements on this point, since the author himself has pointed out how untenable his announced intention is.

The reader of *Adriana Buenos Aires* must also decide how to fit the oddly juxtaposed sections of the work into some type of total context. After pages and pages of hearing about the unhappy lovers, the reader suddenly encounters material of a very different nature. Fragments of metaphysical musings, poems to a dead beloved, aphorisms on art and life, all seem disassociated from the surrounding text. Again, the author is of little direct help to the puzzled reader. His principal introduction, «Nota a la novela mala» (pp. 13-14) comments almost exclusively on the conventional aspects of the novel. Indeed, the only aberrant feature the author mentions is the lack of closure. The novel's prologue mentions that its termination will not meet the standards of «bad» fiction (AB, p. 14). This warning is insufficient to prepare the reader for the final pages of the novel. The structure of the work becomes more loose and seemingly arbitrary until its last pages are a near-random assortment of writings. Commentaries on poetics and on the various characters seem to have less and less to do with one another. A long defense of spiritual over sexual love is evidently sincere, but the comment it makes on the events of the plot is less than clear.

Faced with such gaps in the fabric of the work, the reader must do more than rearrange what has already been committed to paper. Skipping around in the work in search of a greater unity is only a partial solution to the problems it presents. In the Macedonian scheme, skipping is creation, but only at a very low level: «Pero no leer es algo así como un mutismo pasivo, escribir es el verdadero modo de no leer y de vengarse de haber leído tanto» (PR, p. 117).

Thus the reader of *Adriana Buenos Aires* must write for himself the missing sections which will knit together the whole work into an acceptable structure. The material is there, but it is patently in need of amplification and development.

The technique of leaving a work uncompleted exists, then, in *Adriana Buenos Aires.* But its most drastic application is in *Museo de la novela de la Eterna,* the progressive novel to supercede the dying conventions that linger in *Adriana Buenos Aires.* The innovations that occur sporadically in the «bad» novel come to dominate the «good» novel. Whereas the reader of the «bad» novel is only sometimes the secondary author, the reader of the *Museo* is constantly reminded of his authorial responsibilities. The references to the roles of author and reader are so numerous as to take up a large portion of the text. As the author says: «Lo que me ocupa es el lector; eres mi asunto, tu ser desvanecible por momentos; lo demás es pretexto para tenerte al alcance de mi procedimiento» (MNE, p. 248).

The work Macedonio means to do on the reader is this: the training of a new type of reader, self-sufficient and hard-working. This new reader must emerge from the passive reader of «bad» novels, whose powers of invention are in a lamentably atrophied state. Through dialogues with imaginary readers, Macedonio draws out the author latent within each of them. When one fictional reader expresses hope and longing, Macedonio draws him out Socratically: «¿Ser autor?» With this stimulus, the reader is able to formulate the correct response: «Porque me resisto a creer que 'literato' es: quien deja en el mundo todo dicho y nada sabido» (MNE; p. 247). As this fragment of Socratic dialogue emphasizes, no literary act can be meaningful when it flows undirectionally from a creative author to a receptive reader. Literary creation must be a shared venture if it is to communicate meaning; anything less than collective creation leaves «nothing known.»

This is the justification for the author's delegating so large a portion of the book's final elaboration to its readers. One of the first tasks the reader encounters is, as in *Adriana Buenos Aires,* the fabrication of some context for the oddly juxtaposed fragments that make up the work. One quickly discovers the fragments of the «good» novel are not in themselves sufficient to constitute a fully elaborated work. No mere editing can make something coherent of the *Museo's* disorder. The connective tissue of the work must be supplied by the reader himself.

Perhaps the most evident example of this task is the complicated matter of the characters. A number of characters occur in the *Museo,* but they lack the features associated with literary characters by the conventions of «realistic» fiction. Macedonio's mode of conceptualizing and realizing the literary character has been extensively studied by Jitrik.[17] Jitrik finds the Macedonian character notable for its vague and incomplete elaboration. The critic's 1975 inquiry into the progressive dematerialization of the literary character in this century takes its title from Macedonian terminology: *El no existente caballero.* In Jitrik's analysis, such sketchiness permits the character an unprecedented freedom. Corresponding to the characters' increased freedom is the lessening of the author's control.

What interests us here, though, is the way in which Macedonio obliges the reader to devise some appropriate response to these «nonexistent» characters. Clearly, the passive reception of a fully-developed character, while adequate for «bad» novels, is of no avail in the case of «good» narrative. Again, Macedonio is thinking along the same lines as Barthes. Barthes, in his *S/Z,* considers what makes some texts susceptible to a «writerly» reading. His conclusion is that an author can facilitate or abort a «writerly» reading by manipulating five master codes in the text. One of these codes, the connotative, is the one employed to organize themes and attributes into a «character.» Barthes states that an author can manipulate these codes in such a way that there is virtually nothing left for the reader to modify; every element is firmly fixed in relation to the others before the reader even arrives on the scene. In this case, the reader is no more than an idle onlooker as characters are developed, themes appear, secrets are withheld or divulged and so on to a tidily resolved conclusion. Conversely, an author who is willing to allow the reader some control over his reading will allow indeterminacy to occur in the codes. The reader must then assist in determining how the various elements in the novel interrelate and in what way they belong to the rest of the world. While a reactionary author may leave the reader with no other option than to read, the author who is willing to leave many possiblities open in the orchestrating of the codes will have a body of co-writers for readers.[18]

This is Macedonio's goal as he effectively prevents his readers from approaching the characters in any of the traditional «readerly» ways. One cannot simply identify with these insubstantial beings, or even care very much what happens to them. Their lack of recognizable features makes it impossible to situate them in any specific historical, geographical or societal context. If they are to constitute part of some larger commentary on real-world conditions, the reader must do most of the work of enunciating that commentary. The strategies needed to deal with such characters are not those commonly practiced among what Macedonio calls «los buenos lectores de novela mala» (AB, p. 14).

It is the reader who must decide what purpose these vague characters may serve. The author's intervention is minimized. The main part of his task is simply to present the characters, and none too clearly at that. An instance of this technique is a supposed guide to the characters. The author announces «En una novela tan ordenada el lector debe conocer a los personajes. Y han de dárselos clasificados. Los nuestros son» (MNE, p. 85). What follows looks like a general characterization of the fictional beings who inhabit the novel. But in fact, it is no more than a listing, and does not correspond very closely to the characters who figure in the work. Among those listed are Metaphysics, the author, the reader and two characters barred from appearing in the novel because of their unruly behavior. Even when the catalogue of characters corresponds to the contents of the novel, it is still unhelpful. The characters are described in such enigmatic language that the supposed guide turns into a guessing-game between author and reader. The inference is clear: the reader must take the risk and invent the characters for himself, because the author will not do the work for him.

If characterization is a guessing-game in the *Museo,* there are many correct guesses. A multiplicity of elaborations out of the materials contained in the *Museo* is most desirable. Thus, when a fictional reader revolts and demands that the author tell him what really happens to the characters, it is the other readers of the novel who answer him. Readers, and not the author, are to rule on the fates of the characters. The other characters propose a variety of solutions to the rebellious reader's discontent, each of which would result in a substantially different resolution of the «plot.» By their fanciful suggestions, we see that any manner of dealing with the characters is acceptable, so long as it is not the work of an all-controlling author. Grafting the ending of a sentimental novel onto the unfinished *Museo,* interviewing one of the characters to find out what became of him, letting the other readers make up a conventional ending to suit the disgruntled complainer: none of these is deemed unacceptable. However, the complainer realizes his demands are reactionary and accedes to the other readers' urging: «Sé nuevo» (MNE, p. 253).

The incompletely elaborated text, then, requires a creative involvement greater than that required by mere skipping. The text, as written, is unbearably fragmentary. Its empty spaces irritate the reader into filling them in. Missing endings, gaps and silence are confusing, but «Este confusionismo deliberado es probablemente de una fecundidad conciencial liberadora; labor de genuina artisticidad; artificiosidad fecunda para la conciencia...» (MNE, p. 266). Plunged into this productive confusion, the reader must either remain confused or create his own order. In the process of making the text orderly enough and connected enough to be read, he assumes a creator status.

Because of the reader's long-accustomed habits, Macedonio must always be guiding him away from the tendency to accept the text just as he finds it. Readers who refuse to skip and to create their own interconnective passages bring back the stagnation of literature. The fear of such an unproductive reading runs all through Macedonio's work. Recently a Macedonian critic also took arms against the uncreative reader. In his 1975 *Macedonio Fernández: la escritura en objeto,* Germán L. García refuses to supply the bibliographic sources for his quotations from the author. His purpose in withholding this information is to send readers productively rummaging through Macedonio's work in search of a sentence that speaks to them personally. In the process, they will be making their own restructuring of the text and providing a context partially of their own devising. García believes that if he were to tell readers where to find the sentences he cites, he would be committing the same esthetic sin as the all-controlling author of the «bad» or «sterile» novel. He would be deciding the ordering and the context of the fragments at hand. The Macedonian poetics forbids any such decision by an authority figure, because it would deprive readers of the chance to exercise their new-found creative competencies.

Supplying missing endings and contexts is a higher creative skill than skipping. Yet each constitutes a partial implementation of the Macedonian poetics. In each case the author abstains from complete authoring, whether by neglecting to create readable order, leaving his text truncated, or omitting the connective tissue between fragments. The underlying strategy is to confront the reader with some absence which he must fill out of his own invention. By creating conditions of nothingness, Macedonio disconcerts and bewilders readers. Yet he assures them that they can overcome their discomfort if they will trust their own creative instincts. As he says, «El imaginador no conocerá nunca el no ser» (MNE, p. 266).

IV. The Collaborating Reader

The absence of order and the absence of context are productive. The next step, then, is to elicit still more creative activity from readers by means of a more drastic absence yet: the absence of a written text. Here we will look at some Macedonian schemes to liberate readers from the constraints of pre-written literature. The goal of a literature that obviates the need for writing is reader participation. Ideally, the reader would enjoy greater inventive freedom than when he had to follow a written work. He would also be responsible for shouldering a greater part of the labor of creation. In the most demanding forms of nonwritten literature, every reader would have to contribute to the effort of collective creation. Unless everyone participated, there would be no literature at all, either good or bad, dying or regenerative.

Some of Macedonio's nonwritten works hew fairly close to conventional forms of literary activity. For instance, he innovates within the preexisting framework of the literary banquet and the *revista oral*. The latter was a feature of the 1920-40 literary scene and consisted of a gathering of writers to read their «contributions» aloud to one another.[19] Although these activities were already being practiced when Macedonio made his appearance on the literary scene, his use of them is original and corresponds to his overall poetic program.

Macedonio's interest in these literary gatherings has little to do with the creation of an elitist «in» group. Rather, he sees them as a small-scale experiment in collective creation. They represent the beginnings of what could eventually be a regenerated form of literary life involving all imaginatively competent beings.

The aspect of these group functions that interests Macedonio is the high degree of interaction they demand from all participants. Readers and authors are the same group of people. Moreover, even when a contributor is not speaking, he must be reacting to the words of the speaker of the moment. The author of a literary toast or of an oral-magazine article is not isolated from his public. Its reactions become part of the total process of literary creation. The interplay between creative writer and reacting listener is spontaneous, immediate and continuous. Thus the fixed nature of written literature gives way to a more fluid form.

Macedonio emphasizes this more open interaction in the text of his remarks to the *Revista Oral de Córdoba*. He boasts that the undertaking has achieved an unprecedented level of communication: «Nuestra 'Revista'... es la única que ha logrado 'hacerse oír'...» (PR, p. 57). Its success is not due to strenuous self-promotion, but to the active inclusion of creative readers: «y esta especial manera de atendernos, que el público no concede ni a los grandes diarios, nos obliga a corresponderle en calidad» (PR, p. 57). Readers are not alienated because they share the responsibility for creating what they read; authors are responsive to the public because they are face-to-face with it, registering its reactions. The toasts Macedonio makes to his literary friends emphasize the same dynamics. Even in those cases where the author cannot attend in person, his toast makes reference to the communal nature of the literary act of toastmaking. The fact that the toast is being received by a reacting, interacting group of persons is a topic of many Macedonian toasts. The ostensible purpose of the toast, that of praising a man's character and achievement, is secondary to making those present aware of the unusual literary event they are realizing.

Collective creation, though, is only part of the appeal of such enterprises. Orality is equally important in moving readers toward a more active model of readership. Listening to a complexly elaborated literary work is demanding, and idle readers need to have greater demands placed on them. The practitioners of a sophisticated oral literature have «un público rarísimo, quizá el más vivaz y curtido, que hace justicia a este género de autores; mientras la crítica vacila y se confunde, ese público no duda que si el prudente hombre no escribe, de su mal se está precaviendo» (PR, p. 56).

Macedonio's quarrel with «bad» literature turns into a complaint against the written word. Literature does well to obviate the need for a written text, because committing a work to writing fixes it for all time and gives it an authoritative quality. The *Revista Oral*, on the other hand, seeks fluidity, changeability and continual renovation as its highest goals. Macedonio reminds his audience of the importance of these qualities in their shared endeavor. For instance, he proclaims that every session should be an inaugural session, because «El nacer sólo una vez... no rige para las ideas, que viven de rejuvenecimientos no de continuidad» (PR, p. 55). He warns the contributor to avoid anything fixed or official: «La inauguración cotidiana nos gobierna--sin alusión oficial--» (PR, p. 55). A literature that is not committed to paper has less the look of something immutable and authoritative.

Participants in this anarchistic enterprise merit special praise, because they have sacrificed the prestige associated with being the official author of a published work. This fruitful renunciation is the basis of «la nombradía que algunas de nuestras firmas ya gozaban, a veces por el solo hechizo de no haber escrito nunca» (PR; p. 56). Macedonio contrasts the authors of the spoken magazine with the editors of large-circulation periodicals. The latter realize their communication is faulty, but attempt to remedy the situation with massive Sunday editions, special supplements and prestigious collaborators. They fail because they always seek to be more authoritative, as if hoping to intimidate their readers into being impressed. The anarchists of the spoken magazine win over their audience by the opposite tactic: they subsume themselves in collective and almost ephemeral literary labors.

Literary banqueting, despite its conventional and official connotations, could also serve as a liberation from the written word. In his toasts, Macedonio emphasizes the provisional status of his words. The fact that part of the toast may be altered in accord with audience reaction is a frequent topic. Making his speeches as unauthoritative as possible, Macedonio warns that his toast «debe 'apreciarse' como principiando con nada que decir» (PR, p. 63). The more makeshift his remarks sound, the further they move away from the pomposity and authoritariansim that are always a danger to writers. The author constantly calls attention to his oratorical shortcomings and the response these supposed flaws elicit from the audience. At the same time, these are the virtues of spoken communication: its irregularities, false starts, fragmentary and inconclusive development of ideas and the possibility of correcting oneself in mid-discourse. Once more, *frangollo* becomes a useful and fruitful feature of Macedonian art. A mismade work is more productive because there are an endless number of possible remedies for its disorder.

Yet, neither Macedonio's spoken magazine articles nor his eccentric toasts really measure up to the ideal. Though they seek to be open and changeable, they come to exist on the page in fixed form. The very words Macedonio uses to decry the inflexibility and even the tyranny of the written text have themselves succumbed to this process of fossilization. Macedonio's contention that literature should not consist of the enshrined writings of recognized authors has not been heeded by his own devotees. As long as a written text exists, there is also the danger that it will eventually be turned into «bad» literature by overly respectful readers.

Macedonio recognizes this contradiction inherent in his efforts. He begs his listeners not to situate his efforts within the realm of written or official literature, but rather to hold them up to the ideal of perfect silence. Yet he is aware that the written quality of his work will appeal more to contemporary audiences than the unwritten aspect. The author proposes something tentative, mutable and erroneous, but the reading public takes it for something absolute, definitive and perfect. Once more Macedonio is faced with his perpetual problem: «el público se obstinó en utilizarla principalmente para lectura» (PR, p. 26).

Thus Macedonio considers the possiblities of suppressing still further the elements that allow readers to find fixed and standard readings for his works: in particular, the suppression of the written text becomes an avenue of experimentation. The most extreme Macedonian program calls for a literature centered on absence rather than on any existent element of the work. The artistic endeavor focuses on that which is missing: the plot, the character's atrributes and actions, the author's guidance.

Exploring the productive possibilities of emptiness, Macedonio shows a concern shared by many modern literary theorists. Jacques Derrida, in particular, has studied those literary works in which absence, not presence, is dominant. Of greatest interest to Derrida are writings displaying «l'absence de centre ou d'origine.»[20] When the thing that ought to have given the work its central significance is missing, the work becomes extraordinarily productive: «L'absence de signifié transcendantal étend a l'infini le champ et le jeu de la signification (The absence of transcendental signified extends to infinity the field and the interplay of meaning)».[21] This certainly applies to those Macedonian works where there is an attempt to banish every element that might dictate to the reader what the «main point» of the work is.

In our later discussion of irrational and playful language we will see a further likeness between the Macedonian outlook and Derrida's theories. Both insist that the features of language that make it a poor instrument of communication are those that make it a good medium for art. Rather than getting his message across to the reader at all costs, the modern artist may do well to fashion an «idioma de incomunicación» (PR, p. 70). Thus the author pictures himself at work «escribiendo el libro menos entendido del mundo» (PR, p. 70).

What interests us here is Macedonio's utilization of what he calls, variously, simplification (PR, p. 80), literary silence (PR, pp. 63-65) and nothingness (for instance, in *Continuación de la nada*) and absence (MNE, p. 7), this last being the term used by Derrida. For Macedonio, leaving out elements seemingly key to the work is a remedy against the author's ingrained tendency to be authoritative and the reader's equally ingrained tendency to submit to his domination. As Fernández Moreno summarizes:

> Aquí viene lo que Macedonio llama el segundo problema. El estado de belleza artística tampoco debe tener ninguna instructividad o información ni ninguna otra finalidad que si misma. No obstante que la palabra es el instrumento prominente de la información la instrucción, la ciencia...debe obtener estados de ánimos enteramente extentos de noción. No es, por ejemplo, belarte, él ensayismo literario enredado con didáctica o ciencia.
>
> Entonces--se pregunta Macedonio--¿qué queda para la prosa, suprimiendo la narrativa, la descripción, los famosos *caracteres,* las sonoridades, las imitativas fonéticas, las doctrinas o ideas...las enseñanzas, las sabidurías...?[22]

To dispense with the written text is revolutionary, for it is the most authoritative-looking feature of literature. Those who either refuse to learn to read or avoid reading figure among Macedonio's admirable mavericks. Readers who fall asleep, leave off reading or only read dustjackets display a salutary disregard for the author's message to them. Their rebellion has meaning in a society that uses written literature to intimidate and coerce: «Ahí está ese gran pensador que se me hizo odioso desde que quiso encerrarme en el duodécimo paréntesis de su primera página; salté el palito final cuando ya lo estaba parando él y me juré no leer» (PR, p. 117).

Macedonio fancifully situates himself among the illiterates and nonreaders who defy the established order of literature. He has his editor read his contribution to the *Revista Oral* in his stead, with the explanation: «Macedonio es analfabeto: por descuido de su familia sólo se le enseñó a escribir sus *Obras completas*--que será el primer libro que publicará--pero no a leer» (PR, p. 45). Macedonio also claims that he had to take up writing in order to escape the tyranny of reading.

Faced with the oppressive potential of the author-written work, Macedonio praises silence as an esthetically ideal form. Whereas writing a text means limiting the reader, silence offers infinite possibilities. It is a «texto fácil de recordar y del cual el Hablar es la única errata posible.» (PR, p. 63). The author sets a new goal for himself: «no haber dicho nada en suma» (p. 63). Silence is a good model for creators because it is so susceptible to infinite reinterpretation, so receptive to reader input. The blank pages found in misprinted books represent, by this standard, «ocho o diez páginas de heroísmo de autor» (PR, p. 63). Falling totally silent, though, is a very crude assault on wordiness. Literature must develop more sophisticataed techniques: «ese esfuerzo, señores, de transcripciones.»

V. Literature without a Text

Macedonio's above-cited praise of silence is consonant with the rest of his poetics. Yet the claims he makes for its powers are ironic. Merely confronting the reader with blank pages is neither useful nor fruitful. Readers have no skills that will enable them to exploit the rich potential of an empty page.

What must be done, then, is to present a version of the empty page that readers can deal with. If readers without a text are the ideal type, then the innovator must devise ways to wean readers away from their reliance on the printed page. He must know how to incorporate silence into his works in sufficient amounts to be fertile, but not so much as to discourage his audience altogether. In particular, he must increase his public's awareness of empty spaces in art and their esthetic function. Only when readers grasp the point of these innovations will they be willing to produce the effort required to participate in them. The audience for these new works must be created along with the works.

Here, Macedonio shows his kinship with other radical creators of the twentieth century who have worked with the possibilities of silence. Susan Sontag, in her overview of the phenomenon, finds a tremendous proliferation of such attempts: «The art of our time is noisy with appeals for silence.»[23] This abundance of examples permits her to establish an informal typology. Outside art altogether is complete silence, for «As a property of the work of art itself, silence can only exist in a cooked or nonliteral sense. (Put otherwise: if a work exists at all, its silence is only one element in it)».[24] Within the realm of artisitic endeavor, but limited in scope, is the deployment of silence as aggression against the public. This attack is keenly disturbing to most audiences, who tend to see any lessening of artistic communication as «a dismantling of the artist's competence, his responsible sense of vocation--and therefore as an aggression against them.»[25]

Sontag's highest category of silence, and one to which Macedonio belongs, falls silent in order to allow the audience a certain discretion in how the work will emerge. Her models of this tact are the painter Jasper Johns and the composer and vanguard stalwart, John Cage. Cage is especially commendable for his willingness to relinquish the final elaboration of his work to collaborators, fate or the way in which the audience chooses to receive it. Among his more notable efforts are 4'3'', four minutes and thirty three seconds of programmed concert-hall silence, and compositions whose structure depends on a casting of the oracular *I Ching*. Decisions may be made by a randomly twisted radio dial or other mechanical means.

The work of the «tactful» Cage may provide insight into some of Macedonio's more demanding proposals. That is because Cage and his colleagues have had the opportunity to realize their works. Macedonio, on the other hand, did not find readers bold enough to carry out his more «silent» schemes. He concludes that, at least in literature, «del Silencio...el procedimiento de la cita no ha sido hasta hoy encontrado» (PR, 63). Until more favorable conditions obtain, artists must abstain from some of the more «noisy» practices common to their art: «cultivaré en lo posible la No-deificación y el No-empalagamiento» (PR, p. 305) It is interesting that so many of Cage's experiments are in the field of musical composition, for Macedonio saw music as much closer to silence than literature. The brevity and even sketchiness of music were virtues that literature, in its sadly overelaborated state, should acquire (PR, p. 138).

The lack of a reading public able to undertake the more radical enterprises does not stop Macedonio from proposing them. These unwritten works, even if they go unrealized for the time being, serve as illustrations of the new poetics. Macedonio recognizes that his esthetic demands outstrip what the passive readers of today can perform. Yet, if these readers see what the new art could be they may begin to transform themselves. Throughout Macedonio's writings, he reminds us that present literature, his own included, is far from reaching the ideal. His function, then, is to make us aware of the utopian future open to literature and the skills we need to make that utopia real. Present-day author and readers are primitive: «el no-Hacer no es un género en el que se hayan hecho todos los progresos; véase en lo aquí narrado cómo podía enriquecerse todavía en noble género (PR, p. 138) Because his work falls short of the demands of his poetics, he suggests calling it «La Diosa Omisión» or «El Taller del Ocio» (PR, p. 139). The important thing is not his rhetoric, which is admittedly insufficient, but the possibilities inherent in his demanding poetics.

Utopian, indeed, are Macedonio's reiterated requests for the reader to become one of the characters in the work. To ask a reader to become an author is innovative, especially in a society that schools readers to repress their inventive proclivities. Yet, readers know what behavior corresponds to authorship and, though they may object to having to author, they cannot claim they are being asked to do the impossible. Becoming a character in a literary work, though, is a kind of behavior for which we have no model. The literary characters we know are bound to the author's wishes, but Macedonio asks us to reject this notion of character. Jitrik situates Macedonian characters at the extreme end of a progressive liberation of the literary character from author domination. The central thesis of the critic's *El no existente caballero* is that authors become less and less entitled to decide the attributes, attitudes and behavior of the characters they create. The Macedonian character is the most drastic instance of this renunciation of authorial control; Macedonio abstains from dictating what his characters look like, think, feel or do.

Thus the reader who becomes a Macedonian character cannot depend on the author for instructions. He must determine by his own lights how a literary character, himself, should behave. Needless to say, this places great demands on the reader's invention, self-reliance and bravery. None of us, no matter how able he may be in real-world comportment, has developed skills as a character in a fictional work. Yet, Macedonio urges not only the developments of the reader-author, but of «lectores-personajes» (MNE, p. 265). He seeks to convey, by artistic means, «en la psique de él, del lector, el choque de estar allí no leyendo sino siendo leído, siendo personaje» (MNE, p. 41). When the author considers the cast of characters in his novel, the reader figures in their number.

One's initial response to this unprecedented invitation is to assume that it is a purposefully absurd rhetorical ploy. By asking so much more of the reader than is reasonable, Macedonio shows how poorly developed contemporary reader competencies really are. Asking the reader to perform a truly independent task proves Macedonio's contention that reading the «dying» novel has left readers helpless and dependent: «La novela completa, que es la más fácil, la única usada en el pasado, aquella toda del autor, nos tuvo a todas como infantes de darles de comer en la boca» (MNE, p. 262).

Our incompetence in the face of Macedonio's demands is part of their function. Yet, the author seems to consider these invitations to become a character as serious ones. He assures the reader that he has complete confidence in the latter's latent, untapped creativity: «reconóceme que esta novela por la multitud de sus inconclusiones es la que ha creído mas en tu fantasía, en tu capacidad y necesidad de completar y sustituir finales (MNE, p. 262). It is a recurring assertion of Macedonio's that readers' skills can be brought to a much higher degree of competence than they have been. He is optimistic about the reader's ability to create fiction with minimal guidance. The sheer number of the invitations to become a character suggests they are positive encouragement. It would be pointlessly negative to remind the reader so often of his current-day helplessness. Instead, reiteration seeks to wear down the reader's resistance to the seemingly impossible idea.

Making fiction out of real-life persons and settings was a Macedonian obsession outside his written work, as well. Friends and acquaintances recall his schemes for creating fiction using nothing more than imagination and characters recruited from real life. The fictional setting of this endeavor would be real-life Buenos Aires and its novelistic time would be however long it took the characters to elaborate their plot. The authorial voice would be virtually silent; the creator's task would be that of an organizer. Each character, however, would carry a large burden of literary creation.

A number of such projects are reported in Germán García's book of taped recollections of Macedonio by those who shared his conversation. One involved inserting women taken from the ranks of prostitutes into the lives of respectable families. [26] Moreover, he succeeded in giving an ambiguous status to the figure of Isolina Buenos Aires. Apparently Macedonio abstained from making it clear whether Isolina Buenos Aires was a real woman of his acquaintance whom he presented in mythified form or an invention. The author's son believes Isolina began as a real-life woman and became transformed into the title character heroine of *Adriana Buenos Aires*. [27] Also in this category must be Macedonio's campaign for the Argentine presidency, more notable for its imaginative and novelistic qualities than for any real-world efficacy. Macedonio apparently considered giving this nonwritten novel a written form under the title *El hombre que quiso ser presidente y no lo fue*. [28] Other Macedonian recourses for nonwritten fiction include declaring the conversation in progress to be a fictional episode, suggesting people undertake fictional endeavors and referring to known real-life persons as if they were fictional beings. One of the most worthwhile goals of fiction, in the Macedonian scheme, is to make the reader wonder whether he himself may not be a novelistic character.

What all these schemes have in common, apart from their whimsy, is their insistence on the powers of novelistic invention. Macedonio shows that the human powers of imagination are the real substance of the novel, and the only necessary element. What we think of as necessary features of the novel are no more than conventional trappings. The author's creation of a plot, setting, characters and well-defined theme is a response to conventional expectations, not to artistic necessity. Not even the conventions of paper and ink are really necessary. In a truly imaginative literary ambience, fictional works can be created without recourse to any of these devices. Even everyday events such as conversation can be transformed into sophisticated fictional enterprises if the participants, through dint of imagination, impart to them a novelistic status.

Reading about Macedonio's schemes for the unwritten novel, one realizes that the innovator was virtually the only active participant in the endeavor. Those to whom these imaginative projects were proposed reacted as an appreciative audience, savoring the author's invention and recalling his fantastic proposals many years later. There seems to be little evidence of a more participatory reaction to the Macedonian schemes. For instance, Macedonio did not succeed in mounting a large-scale novelistic production with characters drawn from the real-world human race, although he continually invited people to participate in this novel. Macedonio's poetics had outstripped anything people felt competent to do toward its realization. The author had an audience willing to appreciate the novelty and inventiveness of his proposals, but unwilling to attempt them. That task remained for the supremely competent readers of the utopian future. What Macedonio could effect was the raising of the level of reader awareness and ability. His work was to aid in the transition to this utopia of reader competence.

VI.   Moving toward Macedonio's Utopia

In his attempts to reform reading and writing, Macedonio shows himself to be a quintessentially twentieth-century innovator and an accurate prophet. He believes that all literature so far written has committed one especially grievous sin: being «toda del autor» (MNE, p. 262). The result has been a polarization of the creative and the receptive tasks in literature. Readers have grown accustomed to the idea that they are helpless or unimaginative and must have an all-controlling author do everything for them. Authors have grown domineering and have refused to relinquish any of their artistic responsibility to the reader. The reader's invention and imagination have lain untapped for so long that authors have no confidence in it: «Exceptuado yo, ningún novelista existió que creyera en tu fantasía» (MNE, p. 262).

To remedy this unproductive situation, Macedonio allows readers the opportunity to exercise their untried imaginative powers. Indeed, he tries to make a passive reading of his literary work impossible. The strategies he adopts to achieve this goal are, in great measure, the same ones latter-day innovators took up in the same effort to engage the reader's creative faculties along with his receptive ones.

Macedonio's most overt strategy consists of explaining to the reader why he must abandon his slothful, passive reading habits and become a reader-author. Such proselytizing runs through many writings, both fictional and essayistic, of *nueva narrativa* writers. Probably the most famous instance of this didactic effort is the Argentine Julio Cortázar's 1953 *Rayuela. Rayuela* draws heavily upon the teaching of a fictional literary critic, Morelli, some of whose dictates have become much-quoted axioms among supporters of the *nueva narrativa*. Morelli proposes a plan of reforms notably similar to the Macedonian scheme: «Lo que Morelli busca es quebrar los hábitos mentales del lector.»[29] Like Macedonio, Morelli is repelled by the infantile dependency of current-day readers, passively consuming «El libro que se lee del principio al final como un niño bueno.»[30] Not only Morelli's dissatisfaction but his proposed remedies are Macedonian in character. He suggests delegating a number of authorial responsibilities to the reader: the creation of endings, the decision to read or not to read certain portions, the omission of interconnecting passages, the suppression of linear time and any other device that might provoke the reader's active participation in the act of novelistic creation. Indeed, one may well suspect Morelli of being a fictional figure of Macedonio, especially in light of Cortázar's avowed admiration for the earlier writer.

Macedonian theories and predictions find their fulfilment in many of the practices of the new Latin American novel. The innovator complained that he had neither a rhetoric adequate to the demands of his esthetic nor a reading public prepared to cooperate with his program. Yet he was certain the authors and readers of future generations would grow toward the ideal of participatory, collective/creation. The *nueva narrativa* provides evidence that this was a valid prophecy. Readers of Latin American novels of the fifties, sixties and seventies must contribute a vast amount of effort toward the final elaboration of the work. Authors omit endings, contexts, explanations, character development, definitive time sequence and other of the features that make a work seem finished and readable. The reader must supply all of these omitted elements out of his own imaginative resources. In effect, he must invent a mode of reading adequate to deal with the new demands of each new novel.

The Macedonian art of omission even appears, with certain changes, in the Paraguayan Augusto Roa Basto's 1974 *Yo, el supremo*. This novel of undeniable social commentary is yet «open» in structure. Faced with fragments of writing in often puzzling juxtaposition, the reader must elaborate a context which will fuse these passages into some readable, coherent whole. The author omits any evident justification for the amassing of page upon page of egomaniacal ravings. The reader must tease out an overall pattern from this apparent absence of structure. Although the determination of the work's structure lies with the reader, it is not a structure enclosing pure absence. Real commentary on sociopolitical matters exists in the novel. But it is presented in a most oblique and fragmentary manner, through the garbled expression of a mad dictator. Winnowing out the novel's sociopolitical insights from the crazed rambling in which they lie embedded is another of the reader's assigned labors. In presenting the reader with such massive disorder, both structural and thematic, and expecting him to transform it into something readable, Roa Bastos pursues a sociopolitically useful form of the «open» novel. He gives the reader the materials from which a novel can be fashioned, but makes him do a great deal of the actual fashioning.

However, to situate Macedonio only as prophet or forerunner of the *nueva narrativa* is too limiting. Literary history does link his pioneering efforts to the latter-day «boom,» but we must look at his experimentation in the larger context of the twentieth-century creative ambience. If we situate Macedonio in this way, we see his evident kinship with other radical creative figures of the modern era. The similarity between his innovations and those of others may not result from any case of given or received influence in the literary-historical sense. Rather it marks Macedonio as one receptive to the literary-artistic renovations that swept through the general intellectual climate. When artistic ideas «have arrived» or are «in the air,» they may crystallize in the artistic production of many widely separated creators. Their diffusion relies only partially on specific literary friendships or the formation of movements with group programs and manifestos. Rather, a truly original vanguardistic mind such as Macedonio's may draft its own versions of the new ideas, modifying them to suit its own esthetic demands.

In this sense, Macedonio is kin to the many contemporary innovators who have striven to relinquish part of the creator's control over his artistic product. The all-controlling author cedes to the creative figure who provides the actual elaboration. The most extreme instance of this position to be formulated into an esthetic program is probably the surrealist notion of collective creation. Such experiments as drawings or poems created by a group, each member utilizing one section of a paper folded so he cannot see the other members' contributions, are patently within this current. They parallel such Macedonian schemes as sending a group of characters out into the streets of Buenos Aires to create a novel, each ignorant of the others' exact plans yet all sharing the same underlying esthetics.

Other surrealist notions correspond closely to the Macedonian program of esthetic reform. Analogous to the Argentine's utopian vision of the future of art is the surrealists' tenet that, after the abolition of pure expression, the poetry of the future will be made by everyone.[31] This ideal, which has appealed to some recent innovators just as the surrealists formulated it, underlies much twentieth-century innovation in a more generalized or attenuated form. As Octavio Paz points out, it is an exceedingly useful and fruitful notion that can be applied in a number of ways.[32] As we have seen, Macedonio invented a number of partial implementations of the principle as transitional measures toward an eventual utopia of perfectly competent readers.

Thus Macedonio also belongs among those innovators who strive for something less than total communality of creation. These creators do most of the labor of invention, but still demand some degree of audience participation in the final elaboration of the work. For instance, Alexander Calder's mobiles are frequently supplemented by a notice informing viewers to push on the structure and send its components into motion. It is the moving sculpture that constitutes the true elaboration of the work; an immobile mobile is hardly more than a potentiality or proposal. The viewer is thus moved from his passive, «hands-off» stance to venture into the realm of active artistic expression. Like Calder, Macedonio was willing to prepare all the elements of an artistic work but invite the public to put the last touch on it. In that way, the work would belong less entirely to the author and more to the audience.

Also analogous to Macedonio are those who score a music or dance work in such a way as to permit a multiplicity of possible performances. Whether such composers use chance as the agent of artistic decision or allow performers to make choices, they are effecting the renunciation of artistic control that Macedonio counseled. Once freed from the tyranny of an all-controlling creator, the work gains in productivity and in merit, in the Macedonian scheme. Even if it is only fate and not the decisions of another person that determines the form the work takes, the creator has still done something constructive in the Macedonian sense. He has moved away from the utter domination of art by the artist which, for Macedonio, meant aridity of expression. Even more in line with the Argentine's overall reform are those creators who allow performers to share the responsibility for the shape the work will take in performance. The less the creator specifies how performances of his work should precede, the more productive his scores will be. One can see a strong parallel between such performance works and Macedonio's ambiguous, incomplete instructions to his readers as to how they are to perform the reading of his works. Such instructions tax the imagination in much the same way as musical scores, such as those of LaMonte Young, consisting only of general instructions to performers outlining the shape the work should assume in performance. If the Macedonian reader must decipher the author's playful language before deciding how to proceed, that labor is all the more salutary. This arduous task is similar to the effort demanded by, for, instance, the musical scores of Cornelius Cardew, which «are literary texts, which have to be translated between codes (verbal and musical) as well as between channels.»[33] The more effort participants contribute in decipherment, reflection, rethinking of esthetics and in the elaboration of the work, the more art becomes, in the Macedonian term, fertile.

Macedonio is also like other demanding creators of this century in his need to retrain his audience. Obviously, the passive reader of conventional fiction has limited skills in the area of active co-creation. The request to enter a literary work and perform as a character is too alien to his experience to have any meaning. Therefore, Macedonio had to undertake the schooling of participant readers who would eventually be able to perform his most demanding works, such as the unwritten novel. His proselytic labors remind one of, for instance, John Cage's lecture tours and ceaseless championing of his esthetic ideals. Many creators of new art cultivate a group of fellow vanguardists who share the same underlying esthetic and are willing to undertake the realization of endeavors rooted in that esthetic; again John Cage is an exemplary case, with his long-standing collaborative associations. Macedonio, too, tried to inculcate his friends and acquaintances with his radical notions of art as a preliminary step toward his utopian ideal. What he envisioned, though, was a future in which all of the public would become literary performers. In such a utopia, the distinctions between creator, performers and audience would lose meaning.

It should be noted that, while such experimentation has been realized to some extent in other art forms, Macedonio's literary performance pieces have remained unelaborated and, indeed, unattempted. Even readers who appreciate Macedonio's urgings to create a novel by becoming a character in it are unlikely to attempt to implement the suggestion. The author himself sees an element of failure as inevitable in his more radical schemes. He attributes this failure to his own lack of expertise in carrying out the demands of his new poetics and to the relatively unadvanced state of the literary art. Readers, though more competent than they believe themselves to be, are not yet skillful enough for drastic departures from «bad» literature.

In Macedonio's view, readers will only become truly capable when they can function in the absence of all the paraphernalia of the conventional novel. In a whimsical parable, Macedonio describes a refinement in shaving: the gradual elimination of shaving brush, mirror and all the other appurtenances conventionally considered essential to shaving. He then describes his gradual renunciation of everything that makes a collection of art seem significant: works executed in acceptable media, artists' signatures and so forth. Finally he is able to liberate himself from these material proofs of artistry and find imaginative satisfaction in a collection of stray wisps of paper (PR, p. 80). He makes it clear that such an arduous renunciation of official proofs of significance must be a goal for readers and authors. Readers must not rely on externals to tell them a literary work is worthwhile. Literary reputations, critical editions proclaiming their fidelity to the author's intentions, the attribution of a work to a particular author, the insistence on reading a work in its entirety: all these are the marks of an author-oriented and sterile conception of literature. When imagination, participation and artistry become the highest values in literature, readers will lose their need for these materialistic, real-world reassurances that reading is a justifiable form of activity. At the end of this process, they will be so self-reliant and inventive that they will lose their dependency on the written text.

NOTES

1. See especially Gérard Genette's remarks on Borges's projected literary utopia in the former's «L'Utopie littéraire,» in Julia Kristeva, ed., *Figures* (Paris: Seuil, 1966), pp. 130-131. Borinsky points out the applicability of this passage to Macedonio in her «Macedonio: su projecto novelístico,» p. 35.

2. Roland Barthes, S/Z, trans. Richard Miller (New York: Hill and Wang, 1974), pp. 15-16.

3. Barthes, p. 4.

4. Barthes, p. 6.

5. Jonathan Culler, «Literary Competence,» in his *Structuralist Poetics* (Ithaca: Cornell, 1975), pp. 113-30.

6. Bohuslav Havránek, «The Functional Differentiation of the Standard Language,» in *A Prague School Reader on Esthetics, Literary Structure and Style,* ed. Paul L. Garvin (Washington, D.C.: Georgetown University Press, 1964), pp. 9-10.

7. Jan Mukárovsky, «Standard Language and Poetic Language,» in *A Prague School Reader,* p. 19.

8. Fernández, cited in Fernández Moreno, p. 18.

9. Barthes, *The Pleasure of the Text,* trans. Richard Miller (New York: Farrar, Straus and Giroux, 1975), p. 11.

10. Ibid.

11. Ibid.

12. With his term *automatista,* Macedonio pays passing homage to the *écriture automatique* of the surrealists, another attempt to wrest literature from the conscious control of authors.

13. García has taken this aspect of Macedonio's work as the starting-point for his 1975 *Macedonio Fernández: la escritura en objeto* (Buenos Aires: Siglo Veintiuno, 1975). García relates Macedonio's refusal to make his literature recognizably and acceptably literary with the ideas expressed by Barthes in the latter's 1953 *Le Degré zéro de l'écriture.* For García, Macedonian writing corresponds to Barthes's prophecies about the future of literature as it sheds its self-announcedly «literary» features.

14. One should note that Macedonio here uses *vacío* as a term of abomination for the «bad» literature he opposes. More often, he employs *vacío* to designate the new, «good» literature freed of excessive meaning and elaboration. This use of the same

term with widely differing connotations is typical of the author's paradoxical language.

15. Macedonio was seldom as overt as in this passage in his contempt for routinized bourgeois life. Yet, this was one of the aspects of his thought that most attracted the youthful vanguardists to him. The passage cited could easily have come from the many antibourgeois, anticonformist writings published by members of this movement in their newspaper, *Martín Fierro* (1924-1927; Evar Méndez, ed.).

16. Macedonio was here extending into writing a practice he frequently employed in his oral elaboration of the story of *Adriana Buenos Aires*. He should tell friends certain portions of the plot--avoiding excessive linearity and coherence--and then instruct them to continue.

17. Jitrik summarizes the chief innovative features of the Macedonian character in his «La 'novela futura' de Macedonio Fernández,» pp. 153-58. His *El no existente caballero* (Buenos Aires: Megápolis, 1975) shows these innovations as part of the process of opening the closed, authoritarian «bourgeois» novel to create a freer, more vital form of fiction. See also the critic's 1973 *La novela futura de Macedonio Fernández* (Caracas: Universidad Central Venezuela).

18. Barthes, *S/Z*, pp. 18-20.

19. See Marechal's description of this phenomenon in García's book of interviews, p. 71.

20. Jacques Derrida, *L'Ecriture et la différence* (Paris: Seuil, 1967), p. 411.

21. Ibid.

22. Fernández Moreno is by no means expressing an original thought here. Rather, this passage is cited because it eloquently sums up the response Macedonio sought to elicit from every reader. Whether the reader endorsed or rejected Macedonio's overall project, he or she would be obliged to wonder what literature could be without its conventional distinguishing features--features Macedonio considered entirely incidental to the real business of literature.

23. Susan Sontag, «The Aesthetics of Silence,» in her *Styles of Radical Will* (New York: Farrar, Straus and Giroux, 1969), p. 12

24. Sontag, p. 10.

25. Sontag, p. 7.

26. Francisco Luis Bermúdez discusses these schemes in García's interviews, pp. 86-87.

27. Adolfo de Obieta, preface to AB, p. 7. Obieta and Bermúdez (see note above) both link Macedonio's mystery woman with both his fiction efforts and his biographical circumstance. For Bermúdez, Isolina Buenos Aires was probably a mythified version of a prostitute living in Macedonio's boarding-house. Manuel Peyrou (García, p. 77) mentions the same figure, adding that he suspects she may have been the author's mistress. According to Peyrou, Macedonio would only drop one enigmatic hint about her: that she was an excellent manicurist.

28. Obieta, p. 8.

29. Cortázar, *Rayuela* (Buenos Aires: Sudamericana, 1963), p. 505.

30. Cortázar, p. 505.

31. Octavio Paz, *La búsqueda del comienzo* (Madrid: Editorial Fundamentos, 1974), pp. 13-15.

32. Paz, pp. 15-27.

33. Peter Wollen, *Signs and Meaning in the Cinema* (London: Thames and Hudson, 1970), pp. 105-06.

REMEDIES AGAINST THE OVERGROWTH
OF REASON

I. *Vanguardismo* and Irrationality

Macedonio views art as a means for reforming life as well as art. One of art's great corrective virtues is its ability to move man away from what Macedonio scorned most: «el razonar deductivo-inductivo» (AB, p. 53). Analytic thought, despite its great contemporary prestige, strikes him as a faulty instrument for understanding reality. Rather than lead man to truth, logic can help him «obtener anticipaciones fantaseadas del porvenir y... convencerse... de lo que más conviene a sus deseos» (AB, p. 53). Art, on the other hand, forces one to rely on intuitions, which constitute a more accurate guide to life. In consequence, the insights that arise from contemplating an artwork are more trustworthy. While rationalistic discourse yields only «esterilidad» (PR, p. 113), even a poorly-elaborated novel may «hablar quiere, sin embargo, de la vida-misterio, de la vida-pasión en sus entonaciones eternistas» (AB, p. 80). Creators must exploit this power to the utmost, producing works that force the audience to abandon its logical habits of mind in order to respond adequately.

Before looking at how Macedonio acted upon this tenet, one should recognize that he was by no means alone in his belief. On the contrary, Macedonio's distrust of logic marks him as a man attuned to the vanguardistic tenor of his time. To place his attitude in historical perspective, one must consider both the predecessors and the contemporaries with whom Macedonio shared his antirationalism.

Like many cultured and leisured residents of Buenos Aires, Macedonio kept abreast of new developments in European arts and letters. Allusions in his writings attest to his knowledge of, if not always enthusiam for, George Bernard Shaw (PR, p. 307), Count Keyserling (NTV, p. 8), Anatole France (PR, p. 180), T.S. Eliot

(PR, p. 306) and numerous other fashionable figures. However, the genteel obligation to keep current became a passionate interest when Macedonio discovered the ferment of iconoclastic «isms» that appeared in the 1910-20 period. As he mockingly puts it: «Juro... que me dispongo a entrar en el interminable coloquio y controversia o Confusión Universal sobre Superrealismo, Politonalismo, Inconscientismo, Dadaísmo, Posimpresionismo, Neorrealismo...» (PR, p. 306). The often chaotic pronouncements and works of these groups gave Macedonio a confirmation of his own belief in artistic «confusionismo» (MNE, p. 266).

Like his disciple Borges, Macedonio had a Germanophilic and Anglophilic cultural outlook--an unusual one, in a Buenos Aires that looked to Paris for new artistic happenings. It is not surprising, then, that he shows a notable kinship with the German expressionists. Heroes of this movement figure in his own personal pantheon, especially Franz Kafka and Rainer Maria Rilke (PR, p. 86). The philosophers who stimulated expressionism also fascinated Macedonio (NTV, p. 8). His readings of Goethe, Shakespeare, the mystics, Quevedo, *et al.* (PR, p. 96, AB, p. 201) were in the expressionist mode. As René Wellek describes this approach, the expressionists ransacked the literary past seeking the chaotic, the grotesque, the extravagant and the turbulent, while discarding the rest.[1]

What was this movement that so fit Macedonio's beliefs? All «isms» are hard to define, but critical consensus does exist on their chief distinguishing features. Expressionism, despite its sometimes conflicting goals, strikes most critics as a rejection of science and analysis. Wolfgang Kayser, for instance, characterizes these innovators as creators of chaos capable of writing pure «balbuceo» in order to destroy logically-ordered syntax.[2] *The Princeton Encyclopedia of Poetry and Poetics* calls them «irrationalists and visionaries.»[3] A history of German literature unites dadaism and expressionism through this commonly-held tenet: since «the contemporary world was a madhouse,» art must convey «a sense of the paradoxical, grotesque and absurd.»[4] Another classes «the complete Expressionists» by the fact that «in their work irrationalism predominates.»[5]

This irrationalism sought to maintain a human quality in a world increasingly dependent on technology and artificially ordered systems. Many humanists felt alarm over the swift rise of scientific models of research in many areas of human inquiry. In sociology, for instance, essayistic social observation had long been the *modo standard.* The twentieth century brought improved methods of obtaining objectively verifiable data. Consequently, the commentator's personal perceptions and imagination were no longer in the foreground. Technical skill at gathering and manipulating data according to rigorous standards became necessary for successful investigation. Empiricism was also on the rise in other social sciences, in art history, musicology, film esthetics and other areas of study. Worried contemporaries foresaw a future in which the human element would be completely absent from investigations into the human condition.

The reaction to this increase in rigor was, at times, a deliberate return to subjective scholarship, renouncing the available new methodologies. As one history of the period summaizes: «Expressionism was more than a literary tendency; it had its counterpart in almost every sphere of thought... The 'Geisteswissenschaften' in German Universities turned from scientific research and made the intuitive discovery of underlying experience ('Erlebnis') the aim of study.»[6] Works championing man's gifts of imaginative insight found an enthusiastic audience. Henri Bergson's 1907 *L' Evolution créatrice,* for example, «was widely read in Germany and gave this conception an added stimulus. Bergson sought to demonstrate the helplessness of analytic reasoning in the face of the deeper problems of existence. In place of mathematical investigations he preached the need for intuition which is that type of intellectual assimilation by which one penetrates into the essence of an object.»[7]

The demand for greater faith in subjective perceptions had strong implications for the nature of literary representation. No longer was it adequate for an author to «document» aspects of reality as they appeared. Rather, he must offer the reader a version of the world corresponding to his own inner insights and personal understanding. The works that followed from this tenet were, in one critic's words, «an *expression* more symbolic than anything else. In place of the working-out of fictional contexts that could be measured against observable reality, one finds creative visions that were verisimilar only in the most enigmatic of fashions.»[8] Not only was naturalism not art, but, according to this doctrine, it contributed nothing to man's essential sense of himself and his world. What was needed, instead, was a patently mythic, metaphorical representation, very like the way inward man perceived his experience of the world. What rational, objective man saw had no place in the artistic endeavor. As Kasimir Edschmid, the manifesto-writer, put it: «Die Welt ist da. Es wäre sinnlos, sie zu wiederholen (The world already is there. It would be pointless to repeat it.»[9]

As well as being highly metaphorical, the expressionistic work of art was often exceedingly chaotic in its structure and verbal texture. Kayser points to this formal disorder as analogous to the world as the expressionists viewed it. Theorists of the movement praised those works that most blatantly defied standards of cohesion and order. Kurt Pinthus, prefacing his 1920 *Menschheitsdämmerung* anthology, proclaimed expressionism to be «all eruption, explosion, intensity.»[11]

Events brought these innovative currents to Macedonio in the persons of Borges and Gómez de la Serna. Fernández Moreno lays special emphasis on the 1921 arrival of Borges in Buenos Aires, fresh from the European vanguardistic scene.[12] Borges had lived in Switzerland during the days of dadaism, the forerunner of expressionism. His enthusiasm for the latter movement led him to compose verse in Spanish imitating the fragmented syntax and horrors-of-war theme of much expressionist poetry.[13] Although he soon abandoned this direct imitation, Borges continued to envision a kindred Argentine vanguardism to clear away the cluttered rhetoric of literary Spanish. When Macedonio met him, he was at his most drastically innovative and proselytistic.

Unlike Borges, Gómez de la Serna favored no one «ism.» Rodolfo Cardona states that one of the innovator's great virtues was his ability to participate in a variety of vanguardistic activities without forming an affiliation.[14] Rita Mazzotti Gardiol gives an account of the various artistic reformers who worked or conversed with Gómez de la Serna: it includes Tristan Tzara, founder of dadaism, the young Pablo Neruda, the pioneering critic Karl Vossler and others.[15] Consequently, when literary Buenos Aires welcomed the exiled Spaniard, it was also hailing the definitive «arrival» of the vanguardist idea.

Throughout the twenties, Buenos Aires was host or home to numerous experimentalists. Literary historians have described the rather riotous literary scene of those years, characterized by banqueting, feuding, one important «ism,» *ultraísmo,* and, among others, the newspaper *Martín Fierro* (1924-1927). Much of this activity was more enthusiastic than innovative, but it gave Macedonio readers and conversationalists with whom he could develop his dogmas.[17] *A Newcomer's Notes* chronicles his greatest involve-

ment with this movement. The notes show their author col-
laborating in a collective-creation experiment, magazines, the
elaboration of shared theories and hypotheses and the presentation
of tributes to such visitors as the Spanish poet Gerardo Diego and
Marinetti, Italian founder of futurism. Macedonio, long a solitary
inventor, expresses wonderment at being surrounded by seemingly
like-minded colleagues. He attributes Leopoldo Marechal's poetic
achievements partly to this stimulating environment: «la inquietud
profunda y el operar continuo de las almas artistas de Buenos
Aires» (PR, p. 77). However, Macedonio eventually wearied of the
festivities and, according to García's documentation, returned to a
more solitary literary life.

The list of predecessors should really also include the French
surrealists, although the author prefers to claim affiliation with
English, German and Spanish innovators. Surrealists, too, were in-
tent on returning too-rational man «al sueño, al delirio, a la in-
congruencia y aun a la locura.»[18] Of the various chief figures of
this movement, Macedonio especially resembles Alfred Jarry.
Jarry, too, employed whimsy and wild disorder to treat essentially
metaphysical questions. The French writer's *pataphysique* follows
from a tenet that might equally well have been Macedonio's:
«What's really interesting isn't the laws, but the
exceptions.»[19] Julio Cortázar links Jarry and Macedonio as two
writers who used their comic gifts to move the reader toward an irrationalist's view of life.[20]

André Breton, patriarch of surrealism, also has many of the
same dogmas underlying his work as does Macedonio. Especially
important to both is the role language can play in restoring vitality
and magic to modern man's existence. The section of this chapter
dealing with language will show how Macedonio, like Breton,
sought to pull mankind out of its too-well-ordered stagnation by
working directly upon «our powers of enunciation.»[21]

Macedonio does acknowledge a variety of influences from outside his own century. Searching for his own ancestors, he follows
the expressionists' concept: «the most intense writers were the most
valued.»[22] Typical of Macedonio's literary judgments is his eccentric praise and censure of Goethe. In his view, Goethe excelled
at depicting human beings in the throes of intense irrational states:
«Creador de Margarita, de Mignon, ¿cómo pudo callar? !Pasión
idoneidad suprema del Ser¡» (NTV, p. 22). Faust, on the other
hand, strikes him as an unworthy invention, «hinchado de

estúpidos afanes de saber terreno» (AB, p. 201). The Goethe commentary manifests Macedonio's belief that literature must be free of «cómo son las moléculas y qué temperatura hay en el sol» (AB, p. 201). By maintaining a poetic universe uncontaminated by analysis, certain authors win Macedonio's admiration: Tasso, Cervantes, Poe, Sir Walter Scott and, in a paradoxical «mystical» reading (PR, p. 321), Emile Zola.

A second ancestral line Macedonio recognizes consists of authors skilled in verbal ludics and sly nonsense. In this lineage are Cervantes, Mark Twain, Lawrence Sterne, Francisco de Quevedo and the Argentine satirist Estanislao del Campo (PR, p. 49). He also cites a number of negative influences, i.e., solemn, pompous and literal-minded authors. Among these are the pastoral Virgil, «enseñando agricultura» (PR, p. 292), writers of patriotic odes, Quevedo as a moralist, Shakespeare as social commentator; and, above all, Kant, the exemplar of the humorless, graceless, plodding writer. At the same time that he situates himself in relation to his forebears, Macedonio reminds his readers that an innovator cannot be tied too neatly to positive and negative influences: «en los momentos en que uno no sabe dónde ha nacido se le confunde también el nombre de sus inspiradores» (PR, p. 49).

II. Philosophical Discourse without Reason

The most open manifestation of Macedonio's irrationalism is the 1928 treatise that so fascinated Borges, Marechal, Scalabrini Ortiz and others. *No toda es vigilia la de los ojos abiertos* is unlikely ever to find another reading public as enthusiastic as the 1920-1940 vanguardists. Scalabrini Ortiz, for instance, urges all readers of his 1931 *El hombre que está solo y espera* to read Macedonio's work. For Scalabrini Ortiz, the treatise represents an «ataque al intelectualismo extenuante» capable of moving Argentina out of its lethargy. In his overall scheme, the rigidity of European-style rationalistic habits of mind has proven especially disastrous to the spiritual development of Buenos Aires, a city rich in spontaneity and imagination. Macedonio is the great prophetic figure whose philosophy can lead Argentines toward the full utilization of their own intuitive resources. Signaling the correspondence between Macedonio's teachings and his own conception of the metropolis, Scalabrini Ortiz calls *No toda es vigilia* a «biblia esotérica del espíritu porteño.»[23]

Scalabrini Ortiz is only one of the admirers of *No toda es vigilia*. In Macedonio's words, Scalabrini's efforts to publish it is «la culpa que con Leopoldo Marechal y F. L. Bernárdez, comparte» (NTV, p. 11). Moreover, the work comes prefaced with quotations from Macedonio's correspondence with prominent contemporaries. While none of these men overtly endorses the Macedonian approach to philosophy, each recognizes the eccentric thinker as a worthy intellectual discussant. William James writes: «It touches me deeply to find myself taken so seriously by so evidently intelligent a man» (NTV, p. 14).

The book that follows is a hybrid work: a discussion of metaphysical topics using an irrationally-based rhetoric such as one normally associates with creative literary works. It is an attempt to counteract a tendency Macedonio had long deplored. To his mind, the appropraition of philosophical inquiry by rational, professional specialists was a grave injustice to the rest of humanity. This complaint runs through the Maceodonian *oeuvre*. The narrator of *Adriana Buenos Aires,* for example, has difficulty discussing metaphysics with one of the heroines because «un amigo pedante la ha acobardado haciéndola pensar que hay lenguajes e ideas hondísmos e inextricables que no se pueden entender sino en seis o más años de profesor y estudio» (AB, p. 224). In *No toda es vigilia,* Kant is the paradigmatic representative of this evil: «Habrá perdido la pasión del conocimiento efectivo, si tuvo alguna vez vocación mística,... llegó a complacerse en el palabrerío largo» (NTV, p. 91). To this dessicated, overrationalized model of philosophy Macedonio opposes one that is intuitive, whimsical, personal and highly literary.

Of the literary features the treatise exhibits, the most salient is the appearance of a fictional character. The work's subtitle proclaims it to be an «Arreglo de papeles que dejó un personaje de novela creado por el arte, Deunamor el No Existente Caballero, el estudioso de su esperanza» (NTV, p. 3). Despite this initial proclamation, the first few chapters appear as the work of Macedonio Fernández. Onelove emerges suddenly on page 81 to take over the labor of explicating Macedonio's ideas, announcing «Soy Deunamor, que os hablaré, personaje del arte» (NTV, p. 81).

This device would lead one to expect a major structural division in the work between the chapters «authored» by Macedonio and those in which Onelove speaks. Such is not the case. Upon first appearing, Onelove offers the reader a number of enigmatic statements about his peculiar status, for example, «se le asignó su espacio de no existencia en una novela no escrita» (NTV, p. 81). But as soon as he ceases to speak of himself and begins to expound philosophical notions, his voice becomes identical to that of Macedonio Fernández in the opening chapters. Thus he can hardly be said to present a new perspective on the problems at hand. Nor can one take seriously Macedonio's claim that the second part of the book will contain «la íntegra Solución al problema» (NTV, p. 78). While Onelove's first words to the reader follow the heading «Solución» (NTV, p. 81), his remarks are no less ambiguous and open-ended than those of his predecessor. Indeed, when Macedonio again becomes the speaker in the text, he admits that «Deunamor no concluye sus tesis, y en la página anterior calla, pero no dijo todo. Debió creer que lo sabías por haber andado tú tanto entre nosotros y nuestras páginas» (NTV, p. 169). Ostensibly brought in to provide an alternative voice and a solution, Onelove offers neither.

Onelove's function, then, is precisely to baffle the reader by his curious intervention in the work. Macedonio points out this oddity and makes it evidence for his basic tenet that life is not governed by logical causality. In a world full of unexplainable happenings, here is one more: «que se oyese la voz de Deunamor dentro del manuscrito de M.F.» (NTV, p. 169).

Other essentially fictional devices further distinguish the treatise from coldly academic exposition. A notable one, corresponding to the author's rejection of linear time, is the appearance of Hobbes in Buenos Aires. During this visit, the celebrated philosopher accepts an invitation to read an excerpt from *No toda es vigilia,* subsequently advertised as «Manuscrito de Macedonio Fernández que los ojos de Hobbes leyeron» (NTV, p. 45). This anachronism gives rise to an altogether literary display of whimsy. A friend of Macedonio's attempts to discuss Rachmaninoff and Scriabin with the celebrated essayist. Hobbes demurs, not because of any chronological problem, but rather because «No creamos ni sentimos música los ingleses» (NTV, p. 37). The modern man addresses Hobbes using the very familiar Argentine *vos* (NTV, p. 37) and corrects his errors as if the philosopher were a schoolchild. A footnote adds a further touch of ironic caprice. The footnote's author feels compelled to take Hobbes to task for «la reproachable inexactitud de jactarse de conocer las obras y opiones del gran Schopenhauer, cuyo nacimiento es posterior a su muerte (la de Hobbes)» (NTV, p. 41).

To these major structural aberrations one must add the numerous linguistic oddities that mark Macedonio's treatise as a work of creative imagination. Chapter titles are highly paradoxical: a chapter labeled «Conclusión» is notably inconclusive while another designated «Definiciones de ideas y vocablos» discourages all hope of definition. Throughout, the use of key philosophical terms varies wildly. For instance, *ensueño* is Macedonio's ideal state of human consciousness, a psychic condition capable of transcending the illusions of waking (i.e., rational) thought. Yet at times he gives this highly favorable term a negative connotation as in this statement: «No hay más que un ensueño, una irrealidad: la de suponer una Causa a la Vigilia, a la Realidad» (NTV, p. 52). After pages of insisting that *ensueño* is the most insightful state, Macedonio pretends, for just a moment, that he, too, associates *ensueño* with error.

The reader receives many clues that Macedonio's discourse is deliberately playful and literary. Particularly startling is the ending to a refutation of Kant. This passage is arduous reading, for it adds to the intrinsic difficulty of Kant's terminology the eccentricity of Macedonio's wording. Struggling to the end, one discovers the author dismissing his own verbiage: «Esta deplorable dialéctica... no rinde ninguna verdad; la abandono arrepentido aquí y reedito mi tesis» (NTV, p. 127). On another occasion, Macedonio claims to have lost a portion of his manuscript containing examples that would support his argument (p. 118). Among other explanations for his withholding of the promised solution, the author claims that «si he empezado a estudiar el problema antes que el lector, llegaré en cambio a la solución junto con él, pues escribo asociado con el lector en una busca común y cordial preocupándome de que todos los datos estén cuando nos planteemos la Respuesta» (p. 102). These facetiously worded statements remind one continually that the work is more akin to the writings of Lawrence Sterne than those of Hugo Schopenhauer. Macedonio insists that his rhetorical strategy is not primarily an appeal to reason: «Mi pseudo lógica, si se quiere que haya lógica, se constituiría con esta fórmula...» (NTV, p. 153). His persuasion is that of the imaginative writer: «Yo he quedado prendado de la manantialidad de Fantasía» (NTV, p. 199).

Macedonio's ideas are much less original than the elaboration he gives them. He argues against the waking (i.e., rational) mind's conceptualization of time, space, causality and death. Unique human identity is a fallacy: fatality governs events; man can do little to map out or alter the workings of the universe. To buttress these arguments, Macedonio refers to Schopenhauer, Condillac, Count Keyserling, Schiller (p. 29), Emerson (p. 94), Henri Bergson (p. 160) and Herbert Spencer, whose work he reads as frustrated attempts at «mysticism.» His «philosophy» seems immediately familiar for, in Carter Wheelock's phrase, it is «the eternal rival of structured religious dogma,»[24] a frequent resort of fantastic writers and «mystical» essayists alike. Wheelock is the critic who has most thoroughly investigated the literary uses of this doctrine in the writings of Macedonio's disciple Borges.[25]

While Borges is tremendously ironic, though, his mentor appears straightforward. Macedonio's worldview becomes the basis for recommendations about how humankind should behave. Chief among these is the removal of the stigma this culture places on irrationally-derived insights. Western man now approves of the results of reasoning, but downgrades whatever emerges from grogginess, free association, intuition or emotion. But in the author's judgment «Los ensueños...son lo más intelectual y voluntario nuestro» (NTV, p. 65). Consequently, man must train himself to heed these vaguer voices within himself and pay less attention to what his reason tells him.

Concomitant with this change in attitude is a revision of one's expectations toward humanistic and social thought. Macedonio himself provides a model by his nonrigorous reading of famous thinkers. For instance, he finds in the work of Spencer, Berkeley and Hume the constituent elements of an intuitive philosophy. The fact that these men relied on reasoning means that they failed to exploit their best possibilities. In his irrational Kant readings, Macedonio claims to be able to «tomar contacto a cada instante con la suprema intimidad del Misterio» (NTV, p. 88) whenever the celebrated philosopher relaxes his «insignificancias dialécticas» (NTV, p. 88). Macedonio's own readers must approach him in this same spirit. After confessing that he has just written an unintelligible passage, the author reassures readers that they can grasp his thought without recourse to analytical reasoning if they will trust their intuitions (NTV, p. 160).

The prevalent contemporary reading of Macedonio's philosophy was also nonironic. Scalabrini Ortiz, in fact, regrets that its concepts appear in such erratic discourse. In his view, Macedonio's fine ideas lay hidden in a «lenguaje enmarañado.»[26] In fact, Scalabrini attempted to separate the «philosophy» from its playful elaboration. He published a guide to Macedonio's 1928 treatise. This commentary is by no means whimsical but, in Rodríguez Monegal's word, it is «ininteligible.»[27] Scalabrini's nonironic reading of Macedonio and his high regard for the innovator's philosophy is not unique. Germán García's book of interviews records many expressions of faith in Macedonio's metaphysical worth. Most startling is Marechal's statement that he only considered *No toda es vigilia* interesting enough to read. Macedonio's literary efforts failed to engage him.[28]

Latter-day readers may wonder at this contemporary enthusiasm over Macedonio the philosopher. Yet it is consistent with the *entreguerre* fashion for derationalizing and deprofessionalizing the social sciences and humanities. Scalabrini was then developing an intuitive, impressionistic approach to questions of urban studies, education, social cohesion and group identity. His foremost achievement in this endeavor, the above-cited 1931 essay, coincides with his most aggressive championing of Macedonio. Later, as the vogue for irrational inquiry into the human condition waned, Scalabrini drew back from his earlier position. He eventually conceded that social phenomena demanded investigations based on theoretical principles and careful research, resulting in more verifiable conclusions.[29]

Throughout the *Martín Fierro* group one sees kindred efforts. Marechal, another promoter of *No toda es vigilia,* was working on his own fusion of metaphysical investigation with literary rhetoric. His experimentation would result in the 1948 *Adán Buenosayres,* a novel with a heavy component of philosophical dialogue among characters and theological statement by the narrator. Xul Solar, Macedonio's consultant on linguistic matters (see MNE, p. 47), elaborated systems synthesizing mathematics, esthetics, linguistics and occultism.[30] Pedro Juan Vignale and Macedonio shared thoughts on a metaphysical theory of humorous discourse. This theory ignored such objectively verifiable elements of humor as thematics and verbal texture, postulating instead a near-telepathic ideal of «'continuidad humorística' dirigida a un 'interlocutor prohibido'» (PR, p. 108). Macedonio's friend Enrique Villegas collaborated with him on a new musical theory. This discipline, too, was to avoid consideration of that which could be observed and measured in order to concentrate on the spiritual aspects of sound production.[31] As is evident from Macedonio's letters and toasts in *Papeles de recienvenido,* these vanguardists communicated extensively about these projects, reinforcing one another's belief that such efforts could supplant scientific inquiry.

Needless to say, this expected transformation did not take place. The triumph of empirically-based social research and analytic philosophy makes Macedonio's theoretical writings, including *No toda es vigilia,* historical oddities rather than works of continuing validity.

III.   Reasoning Fools and Wise Madmen

Just as the rhetoric of fiction invades Macedonio's 1928 treatise, so his antianalytic «philosophy» appears in his literary writings. As he puts it: «los originales de ambos han estado tan juntos en mi mesa de trabajo...que aconteció trastrueque de carácter entre ellos: el primero, de ciencia metafísica, me ha salido fantástico, y el segundo, una novela, me ha salido verdadero» (PR, p. 98).

Macedonio makes it his rhetorical goal to free readers from their overdependence on rigorous thought. His first line of attack is to satirize «el embebecimiento astronómico y su cósmico correlativo, la adulación de lo microscópico» (AB, p. 119). The first target of his abrasive irony is himself as, at one time, the exemplary fool of rationalism. The young Macedonio appears as a purely emotional devotee of the doctrine of progress: «no obstante mis pocos años yo era ya joven, y, por lo tanto, rico en sentimientos, viviendo intensamente en dolor y placer, era, como todos los jóvenes, materialista y cientifista (PR, p. 54). Like all fanatics, the young Macedonio unquestioningly assimilates the most patent contradictions. Though convinced that «este mundo es casual y casual nuestra presencia en él» (PR, p. 54), he nonetheless feels able to predict the future accurately. The primordial purpose of such a flawed belief system is not to aid in the quest for truth, but rather to provide reassurance. The young man finds a soothing sense of mastery over the unruly, threatening universe, but he must sacrifice common sense to do so. For example, a false scheme of time and progress leaves him and his friends «infatuándonos de ser posteriores al pasado» (PR, p. 54).

To this ridiculous scenario of science-worship, Macedonio jux-
taposes a positive figure: himself in later years. The older man has
halted the hypertrophy of his deductive-inductive mind: «entonces
mi poder intelectual era mucho mayor que hoy» (PR, p. 54). In
return, he has experienced a strengthening of his human gift for
seeing into the heart of all matters. He has no regrets over his self-
transformation: «en mi actitud mística me siento seguro» (PR, p.
54).

Macedonio ranges sympathetic «mystics» against unbendingly
rigid reasoners in a variety of fictional contexts. In *Papeles de recienvenido* and the *Museo*, literary life is the typical arena of combat. The literary newcomer finds he must defend his wild inventions from rule-bound editors, who insist that writings «ocuparan
un solo lugar» (PR, p. 42). In this same camp are readers who demand that literature should serve as reading matter (PR, p.26).
Other villains include directors of libraries, cataloguers, and writers
with pragmatic or doctrinaire goals (PR, pp. 292-93).

The *Museo* confronts one overly-analytic internal «reader»
with the author and the other fictional «readers.» This stodgy
man's powers of fantasy are so atrophied that he needs an explanation for everything that happens in the novel. He seeks to instruct
the author in the rules for novel-writing: «Aquí no hay nada
sobreentendido, todo debe ser contado» (MNE, p. 252). He pro-
tests the lack of logical nexes in the «plot», the difficulty of grasp-
ing what the work is «about» and the author's feckless literary terminology, which defies ordering. While complaining of being
plunged into nothingness, he fails to acknowledge that his own lack
of imagination is to blame. Eventually, he comes to understand
that this attitude is deeply anti-artistic, for it is precisely its
irrationally-based rhetoric that make literature art.

Adriana Buenos Aires presents the same emblematic dreamers
and analyzers in a wide range of conflicts. For example, the narrator, a proponent of intuitive healing, must struggle against the
supporters of scientific medicine. Again, the technicians prove
ludicrously ineffectual and arrogantly dogmatic. After they have
failed to relieve a case of madness, the narrator kidnaps the patient
in order to apply a therapy consisting of metaphysical dialogues,
long walks, chess, roulette and a masked ball. The madman
responds well to this treatment, but other characters still refuse to
believe in its validity. The narrator sums up: «Pero la gente no tiene
fe: cree más en los destructores bromuras y clorales» (AB, p. 87).

The madman himself, once liberated from technical medicine, becomes a representative of the intuitive culture. The narrator discovers in him the ideal discussant for the metaphysical notions «sane» people reject. In the course of kidnapping the man, he is able to sustain the first really satisfying spiritualistic dialogue in the book. Pleased and surprised, he concludes «Es tan poca cosa la locura ante la contemplación metafísica del Ser...» (AB, pp. 118-19). Other characters torment themselves over the madman's condition, worrying that the narrator's regimen makes no sense. The patient, however, takes innocent joy in the diversions that constitute this program. Clearly, the loss of his wits has in no way extinguished his gifts of insight, pleasure, companionship and meaningful discourse. Only his practical functioning as a member of society is a genuine problem.

The narrator finds within himself and his friends lamentable signs of the prevailing rationalistic world-view. Encouraged by his splendid dialogue with the madman, he attempts to have an equally soul-to-soul talk with one of his «sane» acquaintances and meets with utter incomprehension. Greatly disappointed at the man's cold worldliness, he rebukes him: «Qué lindo se equivoca, Sánchez. Usted ha mirado y no vio.» (p. 124). The madman's fiancée, a shrewd businesswoman, awakens a like distaste. The narrator deems her too hard to feel love for her fiancé; at most, she can muster «una amistad sentida, pero también estudiada» (AB, p. 38). Her cool cleverness makes her the negative counterpart of the uncalculating Adriana, the madman's true love. Even the spiritual gifts of Adriana do not prevent her from lapsing into science-worship. Her response to motherhood includes a reliance on the patent remedies newborns generally receive in her culture. The narrator is unable to persuade her of the superiority of self-healing, simply because belief in technical medicine is too pervasive. Introspection reveals that the narrator himself shares the shortcomings of his age. For a time, he neglected his own emotive development: «era todo inteligencia...Y todo me faltaba» (AB, p. 166).

Outside the narrator's circle of intimates, the world appears full of oppressive rationalizaton. For instance, the narrator recalls with pain his subjugation to analytical models of mathematics: «Sin embargo, las matemáticas puras, es decir, sin mesa examinadora, solicitaban mi curiosidad de metafísico después de terminada mi carrera» (AB, p. 180). The reader finds an extensive sample of the intuitive mathematics he would encourage. He develops a system for winning at roulette which is also capable of generating answers to highly abstract problems. The proof that this confusing system works, though, cannot appear in the novel because «el no creer es el primer deber del lector de novela» (AB, p. 184). The entire episode gives a model of how fancy and caprice can be part of endeavors such as mathematics, now subjugated to considerations of rigor.

The book lampoons various groups for their part in enforcing hyperrationalization. In one subplot, a team of laboratory technicians struggles to account for a urine sample with the exact chemical composition of *eau de cologne*. The obvious fact that it is *eau de cologne* seems to elude the hardworking analysts. Astronomers merit derision because «creen que la realidad es misteriosa y además bella porque hay muchos millones de leguas entre astros» (p. 119). Other targets of scorn include agnostics (p. 118), degree-conferring committees (p. 89), origin-of-life theorists (p. 119) and all those who pursue empirically-based research. These last are likened to card-reading fortunetellers, since «Las cartas y la ciencia son más bien ventajosas porque si nos dicen lo que no nos agrada tiramos otra suerte hasta que hable mejor» (p. 54).

Against such an onslaught of reasoned nonsense, man must oppose actions that are anomalous, dreamlike, conveying messages from the hidden side of human nature. The narrator of *Adriana* is quick to point out the nobility of such expressions. His initial skepticism about the madman softens when, for no readily discernible motive, the latter sends his own guitar. The gift touches the recipient for its «enigmática intención» (AB, p. 60) and affords him an object for his meditations. He responds, at last, in an equally intuitive manner by picking up and playing the long-unused instrument at a moment when he must move closer to his troubled, now missing, friend. Adriana is capable of communicating without resorting to any regularized system of signs. On one occasion, she unlocks her door, but rather than enter, chooses to sleep that night on the stone threshold. After making sure there can be no banal cause for her behavior, the narrator interprets it: «la calle le dijo: 'Nada en mí te espera, y la puerta de su hogar: 'Todo de aquí se ha ido'.» (AB, p. 167). Other nobly enigmatic acts include the narrator's refusals to provide any likely-sounding «proof» of his version of events, either to other characters (p. 124) or to the reader (p. 184).

The great underlying irrationalism, though, remains

Macedonio's persistence in writing a novel he recognizes as bad not only by educated people's standards but also by the criteria of the most vulgar reader (AB, p. 185). Writing itself, its structural and linguistic possibilities, displaces moralizing rhetoric as the innovator's chief arm against a too-reasoned world.

IV. Disrupting Rational Reading

The denunciation of analytic reasoning is not in itself sufficient to change behavior. A paradigmatic figure in Macedonio's works, and, indeed, in twentieth-century fiction, is the individual unable to free his mind from obsessive analysis even when he cares to do so. An entire misdirected process of socialization leaves one with the conviction that logical thought is superior to any other type. In *No toda es vigilia,* for example, Macedonio makes himself, Onelove and Kant all victims of this situation. While Kant fails to liberate himself from his era 's demand for rigor, betraying his own mystical gifts, Macedonio and Onelove are able to check their occasional backsliding into hyperrationalism. Catching himself in a too-structured arugment, the author points out: «Hago aquí dialéctica como las que hace Kant, que, sin embargo, en cierto momento, menosprecia la dialéctica. Yo creo que la dialéctica no tiene poder ni siquiera contra la Dialéctica» (NTV, p. 153). The metaphysician continually reminds himself that his praxis, as well as his theory, must be that of a visionary dreamer.

The most patent feature of this pragmatic irrationalism is the bewilderingly fragmented and arbitrarily ordered form of the writings. As the author's son and anthologist observes, every Macedonian text can best be called «Miscelánea, modesta palabra preciosamente connatural al cosmos, Misceláneas mayores, menores, ínfimas...» (PR, p. 5).

Adriana Buenos Aires is especially illustrative of the way in which Macedonio disrupts narrative syntax. The central conceit of this work is that, through a deliberate observance of the conventions of «bad» literature, it will make the further writing of that literature impossible. This paradoxical project was one of Macedonio's favorites. Although he proclaims the possibility of a «last bad novel» without much explanation, the realization makes it clear what this scheme entails. *Adriana* honors the hoariest of novelistic conventions: the amorous triangle, the garrulous and moralizing narrator, stunning coincidences, etc. However, it does so in order to expose and, in Derrida's term, deconstruct these conventions. For Macedonio, the realistic novel only continues to exist because readers have not seen how shoddy its basic premises are. A corrosive irony must show how nonsensical an enterprise realistic novel-writing and novel-reading are.

An instance of this procedure occurs shortly after the events of the plot have begun to «thicken.» Suddenly abandoning its narrator, tormented hero and heroine and various secondary characters, the novel presents an anomalous chapter indeed. Following the title «Mujeres entre flores» (AB, p. 47) the reader finds a listing of feminine names, only one of which corresponds to a character within the novelistic plot. The comments that make up the chapter are not attributable to particular speakers, although they appear as dialogue. This conversation is essentially a collective commentary on death, time, love and poetry. Clues enable the reader to piece together what is going on. Each of the feminine voices expresses a metaphysics identical to that of Macedoino Fernández and the narrator of the plot. Three poems appearing in the chapter belong to the metaphysical poetry of the novel's author. Moreover, one of the women bears the name of the dead wife to whom this poetry is frequently addressed. Clearly, the fragments of conversation, poetry and metaphysics constitute a collage or mosaic of the author's typical thematic material. The fact that this material is so instantly assimilable, even in such an apparently amorphous elaboration, makes an ironic comment on the more structured sections of the text. The entire apparatus of novel-writing as defined by tradition must be arbitrary as well as cumbersome if they can be abandoned without interrupting in the least the fundamental workings of literature.

Even without jettisoning his conventionally-constructed plot, Macedonio creates considerable disjuncture. At one point the narrator, having kidnapped the madman, applies to him with apparent success his singular notions of mental hygiene. The two enjoy a tranquil journey out into the country, conversing with the greatest facility. This happy scene is followed by a different narrator's account of a terrible physical battle between therapist and patient. The two roll in the dirt, employ the most savage tactics and attract a large dog, who inflicts grievous wounds on the spiritual healer. The violence goes without explanaton. When the central narrator regains his usual function, he fails to comment upon this incident other than to discuss the theoretical implication of his self-healing from dogbite.

Jonathan Culler in his *Structuralist Poetics* considers a model for describing this type of disruption in narrative syntax. Certain common expectations exist between author and reader.[32] By convention, the reader expects certain responsible-seeming behavior from the author, particularly in the structuring of plot. If the author has maneuvered his characters into a particular situation, he ought reasonably to continue the action in a logical sequence from this situation.

This is precisely what Macedonio refuses to do with numerous components of his plot. The state of mind of the madman, to give one element, seems not to follow any discernible course of improvement or degeneration. Sometimes the reader learns that the madman is enjoying a remission of his derangement under the narrator's guidance; at other times he exhibits the same disorder as always; sometimes both his whereabouts and his condition are unknown. Near the end, one finds the toneless pronouncement: «Adolfo no ha curado ni curará» (AB, p. 233). Even odder is the narrator's apparent equanimity about this fact, given his profound involvement in the effort to combat the man's insanity.

Germán García has commented upon another broken thread in the plot: the narrator's degree of sexual involvement with the various heroines. In García's analysis, the reader only knows about this matter through the highly unreliable comments of the narrator, who makes a poor case for his own alleged physical and spiritual purity. Two of the young girls he befriends spend one night each in his bed. Another protegee undresses at his behest; his interest, he claims, is in understanding her soul. The narrator recognizes his growing reputation as a lecherous old man. Moreover, he makes statements that cast doubt on his nobility of spirit: «Diré de paso que este amigo por ese tiempo mezclóme en la aventura más curiosa y fuerte que haya ocurrido en los balnearios en conexión con el juego, de la que no hablaré más porque no se creerá nunca en mi inocencia» (AB, pp. 180-81). García views this ambiguity as a sign of the inner conflicts of the biographical Macedonio Fernández.[33] A more structural critic would see it as part of the massive illogic with which the work assails the reader.

Rupture becomes increasingly prominent as the plot progresses. The text becomes the object of a number of commentaries, appended as footnotes. Most of these are either unsigned or signed «author», and assess the «badness» of the «last bad novel.» At times the author proclaims success: «Aquí novela mala» (AB, p. 144). Others are wildly capricious, as when the author claims to be making his very first use of contrived coincidences. This claim is nonsense, for the novel has a plot full of improbable twists of fate. On one occasion, an «outside evaluator» is brought in to survey the progress of Macedonio's project. His verdict is that the work contains a good supply of clichés proper to old-fashioned bad novels, but «por los largos capítulos de erudición matemática, psicológica, metafísica y médica, pertenece a las malas» (p. 185). Still other footnotes question the wisdom of the entire endeavor, point out the many creaky plot devices or simply jeer at the general stodginess of plot and language. The result is that the reader is constantly aware of the ongoing «deconstruction» of novelistic conventions. How seriously he should take this labor of destruction remains uncertain, for each footnote suggests a slightly different opinion on the possibility of exterminating «bad» fiction.

Footnotes and intercalated comments also serve to call into question the autonomy of the fictional narrative. The narrator-participant has a name of his own, Eduardo, but the novel is full of suggestions that he is really an avatar of Macedonio Fernández. Eduardo shares his creator's living habits, friends, musical tastes and voices the Macedonian dogmas. The footnote-writing «author» claims that his protagonist's torment in his own. After a particularly confessional-sounding passage, he appends this note: «Consentidme hacer de literato autor misterioso; hago la novela de otros y quisiera novelarme a mí mismo, en compensación» (p. 181). Intercalating a special note before Chapter Nine, the novelist again creates the illusion that his work is losing its autonomy and merging with his life: «Lo que sigue bajo el título de Ruleta poco interesa a mi relato; su inserción me ha sido impuesta por el despotismo que ejerce sobre nosotros todo lo que realmente se ha vivido» (p. 177).

Antithetical footnotes emphasize the hermetic closure of the novel, its status as created verbal object. Here the author stands outside his product and examines it for its structural strengths and weaknesses. As detached, ironic observer of his finished construction, he makes this remark on one of Eduardo's speeches: «Qué vergüenza, en 1922, yo creía que estaba haciendo una gran novela» (p. 214). He treats Eduardo's speech as a fiction he has constructed, however poorly, and not as an unmediated transcription of his own thoughts.

García points out these opposing sets of remarks, but concludes both sets can be read as part of a psychiatric document. For him, the key to the contradiction is Macedonio's inability to stop writing a novel he knows to be bad, simply because it satisfies a neurotic need. The author's actions are irrational because they have escaped his control.[14] More intrinsically, one can see *Adriana* as a contrived literary experiment, the playful «bad» novel, and, at the same time, a passionately autobiographical statement. Rather than hide the paradoxical character of his (and all) literary creation, the author puts it in the foreground with his inconsistent self-commentary.

The novel's ending reduces narrative syntax to utter garble. The narrator-Macedonio declares himself too exhausted to write the last two chapters. The work's autonomy wavers again as the reader receives, in lieu of constructed chapters, «los esquemas que tenía hechos. Que el lector se afane en dar plenitud a ambos capítulos: yo lo incito a autor» (AB, p. 231). What follows is a series of cryptic jottings, e.g., «El amor ha sido cercado por la tristeza, y languidece. La Muerte hace la tragedia del amor: la Locura?» (AB, p. 233). Again, the elements of the plot refuse to fit into a logical pattern. Borges and Scalabrini Ortiz, formerly included in the references among the literary friends of the authorial Macedonio, now join the cast of characters from the lachrymose plot. One of these fragments has the narrator and all his friends and literary creations participating in the solemnly ritualized «lanzamiento de una cortesana» (AB, p. 232). Shortly afterwards the reader finds the narrator denying that physical love can have either artistic or moral value. In sum, the «weary» Macedonio has contrived to present the reader with the pieces of a puzzle that will not admit a solution: a final dereliction of «reasonable» authoring.

V.   Language Placed «Under Suspicion»

Language itself becomes a target of Macedonio's massive campaign of irrationalism. Logical sentence structure, as mankind's most intimate, internalized rational structure, cannot remain exempt from the innovator's disruption.

In Macedonio's teachings, language as subversive expression has special importance. His ideal of literary expression uses the real-world tongues of man, but with one important modification:

«no les restará más defecto que el de 'Hablar siempre'» (PR, p. 164). That is to say, language will cease to be the vehicle by which the speaker hopes to convey some message of overriding importance. The anarchistic possibilities of this «silenced» language present the imaginative writer with unlimited opportunities. Macedonio encourages the exploitation of «sinonimia, que es una cómica riqueza» (PR, p. 309). Authors merit applause when they utilize the chaos latent within language to bring forth «libros ininteligibles» (PR, p. 70). Gómez de la Serna provides a model of this unintelligibility by suppressing any context that might give too fixed a meaning to his metaphors (PR, p. 105). By virtue of his rejection of the «poema construido,» the Spanish author achieves Macedonio's goal of «mystic» art (PR, pp. 105-06). Xul Solar, too, is a hero of linguistic illogic; Macedonio describes his friend's work as a «taller lingüístico» (MNE, p. 47) in which language is continually being deconstructed and reconstituted in new and ever less communicative ways. The end result of Xul's tinkering is a «lenguaje de incomunicación» (PR, p. 310) whose beauty and richness serve no vulgarly pragmatic end.

In preaching the systematic breakdown of language, Macedonio shows his alignment with twentieth-century vanguardism worldwide. Walter H. Sokel characterizes this line of renovation: «We are here at the crux of the problem of obscurity in Expressionist and, in general, much of modern writing. Art is no longer communication.»[35] Kayser writes of the expressionistic «rotura de todos los vínculos lingüísticos» resulting in, often, unintelligibility.[36] Surrealism, too, made manifest the distance between verbal formula and any possible meaning:

> The surrealist poem is... a locked, reflective universe where language exists, to suppose the impossible, on its own terms (as Breton put it once, 'words make love to one another'), conveying no feeling, no experience, no image felt, experienced or imagined outside itself... Hence Breton's doctrine of 'objective chance': the ellipses, the absence of rhetorical connectives, the dislocated clichés, the unforeseen meeting of rationally unjuxtaposable words. Or sometimes the loneliness of a single word drumming through the poem, pivoting on itself in puns or disintegrating into its syllables forms a material cryptogram of one's 'mental matter, not a transparent sign dissolving into significance but a crystalline thing fixedly reflecting itself ('not

oriented toward anything, just oriented, like a pearl,' as Conc-
teau described Jules Lemaítre).[17]

Another significant parallel exists between Macedonio and the
poststructuralist theories of Derrida. Writing some fifty years
after the Argentine, Derrida posits the same ideal of «silenced»
literary language in which the author makes no attempt to force a
message through the medium of words. For Derrida, the goal is

> the point where language invades the universal problematic
> field; at that point, in the absence of a center or origin,
> everything is turned into discourse--so long as we understand
> this world--that is, a system in which the central signified,
> either one from some origin or a transcendental one, is never
> absolutely present outside a system of differences. The absence
> of a trancendental signified extends to infinity the field and the
> interplay of meaning.[18]

For Derrida, as for Macedonio, the writer has a special responsibility to correct the reader's culturally-induced trust in language
as a conduit of meaning. The emptiness of discourse must be made
so patent as to be unmistakable. Areas where language is an
altogether distorting or unreliable messenger should stand out in
literary writing, alerting readers to kindred dangers in all human
speech. Unless writing performs this warning function, man will
continue to take it for a «jeu *fondé,* constitué depuis une im-
mobilité fondatrice et une certitude rassurante (well-grounded
game, set up on a fixed, firm foundation and a reassuring
certainty).»[19]

The most commented-upon form of linguistic illogic in
Macedonio's work are the *ocurrencias,* sentences containing a
memorable flaw in reasoning. Akin to the *greguerías* of Gómez de
la Serna, the *ocurrencias* violate standard notions of time, space
and casuality. The best study of these sentences is the stylistic
analysis of Ana María Barrenechea. She finds Macedonio to be using such jarring procedures as the quantification, comparison and
temporal measurement of nothingness. By assigning to nothingness
«todos los atributos posibles,»[40] he shows how language can
disrupt orderly thought as easily as it can promote it.

Here are some typical Macedonian *ocurrencias:*

La Novela Inexperta... se atarea en ir matando por separado a «personajes», ignorando que seres escritos mueren todos en un Final de lectura (MNE, p. 21)

Fueron tantos los que faltaron que si falta uno más no cabe (PR, p. 153).

Era tan obstinado y de mal gusto que hasta un instante antes de morir, vivía (PR, p. 153).

Era tan feo, que aun los hombres más feos que él no lo eran tanto (PR, p. 153).

Innovación de una autobiografía hecha por otro (PR, p. 286).

Autobiografía de un desconocido hasta el punto de no saberse si es él (PR, p. 131).

Apresúrate: nos va a faltar tiempo para perder el tren (PR, p. 330).

He tomado pasaje para ir a un país a descubrir (PR, p. 151).

These highly visible infractions of logic put the process of derationalization in the foreground. However, Macedonio also cultivates more subtle and covert forms of linguistic deviance equally fraught with disorder.

Synonymy, ambiguity and lexical gaps attract Macedonio for their revelation of language's deficiencies. Ironically assuming the pose of a fussy rhetorician, he delivers a mock sermon on these impurities. In conclusion, he jestfully sets forth a drastic reform: «eliminar cosas con muchas palabras y cosas sin ninguna» (PR, p. 310).

Macedonio's own strategy is less Draconian. He exacerbates the existing frailties of language. His readers must see that human discourse is a ramshackle device for transmitting messages. Once people begin to view language with greater suspicion, they will see, in Derrida's phrase, that «Il n'y aura pas de nom unique... Et il faut le penser sans nostalgie... (There won't be just one name for anything... And one must face this thought without wanting to turn back...).»[41]

The creation of new terminology allows the innovator to carry synonymy to an absurd extreme. Macedonio's poetic ideal, for example, is, at various times, *Belarte, Belarte-Palabra, Literatura, Prosa, lo bueno, el Arte Futuro* and *la Poemática del Pensar.*[42] One's first reaction, as part of what Derrida scorns as the logocentric culture, is to assign each term a slightly different meaning. This attempt fails for, as Macedonio readily admits, his theory has only two genres: good and bad. Each neologism in his

tangled theoretical discourse can only replicate one of the two. [13]
Simple binarism also underlies Macedonio's exuberantly
redundant metaphysical jargon. At the positive pole is the
unanalytic vision of life, at the negative, the scientific world-view.
His *summa bonum* becomes, from page to page, «la vida-misterio»
(AB, p. 80), «vida-pasión» (p. 80), «misterio del Ser» (p. 117),
«visión» (p. 127) and «lo que se sueña» (p. 117.) Certain words
would seem to refer both to the positive and the negative vision,
e.g., *inteligencia, locura, embebecimiento* and *ensueño*.

Adding to this terminological muddle is the fact that the true
expression of Macedonian concepts cannot use human language.
The author draws attention to the essential hopelessness of his task
in *No toda es vigilia:* «Justo es decir que a mí me ocurrirá la
necesidad de suprimir las palabras estados, subjetividad, Ser, porque en mística todo es estado, todo es subjetivo, todo es Ser; nada
hay que no sea ellos, diferente de ellos, y por tanto no se les puede
'nombrar'» (NTV, p. 107).

The verbal texture of the author's work exaggerates this
hopelessness, discouraging the search for fixed meanings. An example of his disordering is a footnote (NTV, pp. 159-60). Syntactic
and semantic difficulties assail the reader in the first sentence: «Me
inspira, indudablemente, en la frase, no en el pensamiento, el
magnífico e infidente, con el público, no conmigo, Schopenhauer.»
A disconcerting syntactic contortion has wrenched subject and
predicate far apart. Separating them is a jumble of words including
three adverbial «asides,» two A-not-B structures and two very
disparate adjectives describing Schopenhauer. Even after identify-
ing all constituent elements and matching modifiers to referents,
one still cannot grasp its meaning readily. Macedonio seems to be
saying that he appropriates Schopenhauer's verbal formulae
without sharing the underlying philosophical vision. This would be
poor behavior for a disciple. No doubt, the sentence is a showily
faulty expression of quite another proposition: Macedonio uses
Schopenhauer's phrasing to express an idea the former had
discovered independently. The sentence also sets up an impossible
privileged relationship between these two. Schopenhauer can
reasonably be «faithless» to the public, a constant, universal entity
capable of being misled or betrayed regardless of time, place, or
degree of personal contact. An individual, though, cannot hope
that his assiduous reading of Schopenhauer will move the
philosopher to single him out for preferential treatment.

The second sentence continues to play on this confusion of interpersonal and author-public relations. Macedonio starts with a conventional figure of speech that could easily be used by a chatty author in order to establish a tone of pseudointimacy: «al despedirme de mi leyente y de él (Schopenhauer).» However, the metaphorical «coziness» between Macedonio and his mentor soon takes on a ludicrously literal character. During their latest «gloriosa visita,» Macedonio reports, the two consumed a good deal of bitter *mate* tea. The original confusion of readership and friendship is compounded when Macedonio begins to use the language of business transactions as well. He recalls: «hice conocer Bergson al pensador Malagarriga a cambio de regalarme él a Schopenhauer; villano negocio... hice con el amigo.» This humorous chaos makes nonsense out of the author's favorite ideas: the opening of literature to reader input and the opening of every written work to every other.

Verb forms exhibit the same randomness. The main verb of the second sentence occurs twice, once on each side of a lengthy parenthetical digression. On its first appearance, it is in the present tense; on its second, superfluous appearance, it is in the past. This fluctuation between present and past forms is a correlative of Macedonio's rejection of linear time, a major theme of the book.

The chief structural strategy of the second sentence is delay, keeping the reader from reaching the «punch line» by putting redundancies and digressions in his way. The reader awaits a revelation of what Macedonio told Schopenhauer the other night. But he must twice perform the labor of reading not only the main verb but also the expression immediately following it. Omitting the intervening parenthetical aside, one pieces together this tautology: «al despedirme de mi leyente y de él... no pude menos de despedirme de él.»

Further impediments to the reader's progress include the completely unnecessary clarification and amplification of a possible ambiguity. *Amargo* can be either an adjective meaning *bitter* or a noun meaning *bitter mate herb brew*. The chances of any reasonably competent reader confusing the two are very slight, indeed. After all the linguistic chaos Macedonio has inflicted on his reader, it is an absurd irony that he should choose to explain, in such detail, a pseudoproblem. Here communication has gone completely astray: the speaker cannot even judge which features of his discourse will perplex his reader.

This capricious effort of explanation leads the speaker into yet more asides. With each new clause, Macedonio enters a new, quasi-aphoristic reflection, e.g., «sólo el amor iguala o es igualdad que merezca nombrarse.» Commas, semi-colons and colons separate these musings one from the other without signaling any close logical relation. These meditations seem better suited for inclusion in a common-place book than within the structure of a single sentence.

Just before the reader reaches the long-deferred, anticlimactic revelation (an objection to Schopenhauer's use of 'I'), an asterisk appears. It refers the reader to a second footnote (p. 160) commenting upon the first. Here Macedonio cheerfully points out the shoddy construction of the two digressive sentences. He confesses to making himself «intricadísimo» and swamping the reader in «paréntesis confundidos» and downright «erratas.» However, far from repenting of his syntactic oddities, he proclaims them a superior form of discourse. The well-constructed utterance, in his view, does nothing to upset the reader's fixed notions of linguistic or real-world logic. The author should build spectacular flaws into the verbal texture of his work in order to frustrate any naively rational reading. When one cannot reason out the author's intended meaning, he learns to create his own significance. The author's voice falls silent amid a profusion of nonsense: «Aquí pueden más erratas que autores.» Derationalization, then, serves Macedonio's constant goal of relaxing the author's control over literature.

Commentators of the *nueva narrativa* have frequently cited Macedonio as an originator of the illogical vein in the latter-day movement. Borinsky, for instance, sees an absurdism common to the elder writer, Borges, Adolfo Bioy Casares, Cortázar and the «post-Cortázar» generation of writers.[44] Angela B. Dellepiane places Macedonio's «Ilógica del Arte» at the very beginning of the so-called «boom» and extending its influence to the most recent of Argentine novelists.[45] In García's interviews, Macedonio's friends are quick to spot his influence in the more wildly nonsensical passages of *nueva narrativa* writings.[46]

One should make clear, however, that the Macedonian legacy of irrationalism goes beyond a passion for making nonsensical remarks. As Manuel Peyrou observes, the innovator's strategy of illogic grew out of his deep humanistic concerns.[47] To see the continuation of his antirational campaign, one must look at not only nonsense and whimsy, but all manner of prointuitive statements and rhetorical devices in a wide variety of literary contexts.

The most celebrated works of the «new novel» exhibit an attitude toward analytic reasoning very close to Macedonio's. An example of an altogether serious novel in this vein is the 1960 *Hijo de hombre,* the work of a Paraguayan exiled in Buenos Aires, Augusto Roa Bastos. In this work, a compulsive reasoner is the least attractive and least efficacious character. His ability to formulate logical statements about the reality around him fails to provide any meaningful insight or moral orientation. On the contrary, he is able to rationalize away a number of remiss actions and unwise decisions. The irresponsible reasoner betrays the novel's authentically heroic revolutionary, an individual who can hardly be said to think at all. Here the reasoning activity of the mind inhibits the capacity for true perception and right conduct.

The invalidity of analysis is a recurring theme of Roa Bastos's. The narrator of one of his short stories is able to reconstruct the history of a terrible incident of government repression, relying on his well-trained memory and orderly habits of mind. After achieving this historian's feat, though, he realizes his clear thinking is useless, since he has no way of acting upon it. As David William Foster observes, this analytical man is in no way superior to the local peasants who have misconstrued the events completely.[48]

Julio Cortázar's 1963 *Rayuela* is another celebrated instance of this opposition between rationalizers and intuitive types. The reader's empathy goes to the main character's girlfriend, a woman incapable of organized thought but gifted with imagination. The hero has the opposite approach to life: everything must be reasoned out. Able to grasp the nature of his insufficiency, he is yet unable to stop his mind from its ceaseless labor of analysis. In words strongly reminiscent of the Macedonian denunciation of ratiocination, he compares himself unfavorably with his free-spirited girlfriend:

> Hay ríos metafísicos, ella los nada como esa golondrina que está nadando en el aire... Yo describo y defino y deseo esos ríos, ella los nada. Yo los busco, los encuentro, los miro desde el puente, ella los nada. Y no lo sabe, igualita a la golondrina. No necesita saber como yo, puede vivir en el desorden sin que ninguna conciencia de orden la detenga.[49]

Yet another manifestation of this distrust of reason is Ernesto Sábato's 1961 *Sobre héroes y tumbas.* In this novel, the character who brings only reason to bear on reality is a paranoid schizophrenic, a demonic individual who destroys those around him. Some nonanalytic approach to existence appears necessary to achieve even a modicum of happiness. Two characters within the novel reason themselves into spiritual crises from which they only emerge by developing «algo así como una absurda metafísica de la esperanza.»[50] Again we see the Macedonian tenet that the only workable metaphysical system is one that bypasses logic and linear thought.

Macedonio's antilogical stance toward language is also closely akin to that of *nueva narrativa* authors. Cortazar's *Rayuela* is full of tinkering with the workings of language and communication. For instance, an erotic scene is written in a language resembling Spanish only enough to give the reader an approximate notion of what is occurring.[51] The reader encounters pages of inane metaphysical ponderings by the more cerebral and articulate characters. The forced cleverness of these discussions contrasts with the intuitive heroine's expression. Her statements are often deficient in logical meaning, but succeed in communicating in an oblique fashion. She tells her too-logical lover: «vos sos más bien un Mondrián y yo un Vieira da Silva.»[52] Cortázar complies with the Macedonian precept that the great writer is one «que no deja hablar mal a los idiomas» (PR, p. 164). He, too, gives nonsense a place in the verbal formulation.

Less than communicative language is the most startling feature of many new novels. But even more jolting is critical discussion in which meaning is conveyed only obliquely. Severo Sarduy, for instance, has published articles of criticism in a language full of puns, cryptic jokes and a display of whimsy.[53]

Macedonio's kinship with recent Latin American writing is a quasiancestral one. Leaving aside literary-historical questions of prefiguaration or influence, we find that other parallels are equally evident. One is with the writers of the theater of the absurd. In one critic's summary:

> Ours may have been the first extended avant-garde period to have arranged, at the outset, to lapse into its own silence, the first to use the word to get rid of the word.
>
> Go back another ten years, roughly to the coming of Samuel Beckett and the non-coming of Godot. Beckett was of course a literary man, producing literary works; thus far our

avant-garde began much as any earlier avant-garde period. Beckett had a message. The message was that there was no message... If existence had any meaning at all, it was not going to be conveyed to us in words...

Ionesco hit harder, and less poetically. In 'Rhinoceros,' he parodied logic baldly, scoffing at the possiblity that a syllogism could conceivably have meaning for us. Not content with dismantling verbal structures, he attacked not only the world in the gibberish of 'The Chairs' but even the individual letter that went to make up the word: in 'The Lesson' he questioned the sanity of anyone who thought that 'f' was pronounced 'f.' Some of this was mild fun, to be sure, but one conclusion was inescapable: human beings were incapable of communicating with each other through language.[54]

Whether it occurs in the form of antirationalistic pronouncements, the fusion of philosophy with unstructured meditation, the illogical ordering of the literary text, the formulation of logically defective sentences or through the exploitation of the inherent disorder of language, Macedonio's strategy aims at one goal. That is to awaken mankind to the untapped wealth of its irrational powers of mind. Like many innovators of this century, Macedonio rejects the idea that logic can rule over all aspects of human existence. To save his readers from falling into this false belief, he is willing to employ the most deviant form of expression available to him.

Yet, the attack on excess reason is essentially a negative or purgative effort. It should be remembered that Macedonio is an especially hopeful writer with a deep commitment to improving mankind's lot in the future. When he makes readers despair of science, reason and the communicative efficacy of language, he offers them a positive alternative. In the next chapter we will see what he holds out in the way of a utopian future for society, art and language. Just as our author belongs among the modern denouncers of reason, he also can take his place among the twentieth-century prophets of an imaginative utopia.

NOTES

1. René Wellek, «The Concept of Baroque,» in his *Concepts of Criticism* (New Haven: Yale, 1965), p. 76.

2. Kayser, *Interpretación y análisis de la obra literaria,* 4a. ed. rev. (Madrid: Gredos, 1961), p. 193.

3. Entry for «Expressionism,» in the *Princeton Encyclopedia of Poetry and Poetics* (Princeton: Princeton University Press, 1965), p. 267.

4. Henry Hatfield, *Modern German Literature* (New York: St. Martin's Press, 1967), p. 68.

5. Richard Samuel and R. Hinton Thomas, *Expressionism in German Life, Literature and the Theater* (1910-1924), (Philadelphia: Albert Saifer, 1971), p. 62.

6. Samuel and Thomas, p. 124.

7. *Ibid.*

8. Foster, *Unamuno and the Novel as Expressionistic Conceit* (Hato Rey, Puerto Rico: Inter American University Press, 1973), p. 7.

9. Kasimir Edschmid, cited in the *Princeton Encyclopedia of Poetry and Poetics,* p. 267.

10. Kayser, p. 230.

11. Kurt Pinthus, cited by Hatfield, p. 60.

12. See Fernández Moreno, pp. 21-22. Rodríguez Monegal in his «Macedonio Fernández, Borges y el ultraísmo» stresses this connection also.

13. See de Torre, «Para la prehistoria ultraísta de Borges,» *Cuadernos hispanoamericanos,* 169 (1964), 5-15.

14. Rodolfo Cardona, *Ramón: A Study of Ramón Gómez de la Serna and his Works* (New York: Eliseo Torres and Sons, 1957), p. 26.

15. Rita Mazzetti Gardiol, *Ramón Gómez de la Serna* (Boston: Twayne, 1974), p. 21.

16. See, in particular, Prieto's preface to his *Antología de Boedo y Florida* (Córdoba, Argentina: Universidad Nacional de Córdoba, 1964), pp. 7-35, and Marechal's discussion with García in the latter's book of interviews, pp. 67-75.

17. Both Rodríguez Monegal in his «Borges, Macedonio Fernández y el ultraísmo» and Lafforgue in his «La narrativa argentina actual» discount the vanguardists as influences on the older author. In Lafforgue's judgment, the *ultraístas* were unable to comprehend Macedonio's program of reform.

18. de Torre, *¿Qué es el superrealismo?,* 2a. ed. rev. (Buenos Aires: Columba, 1959), p. 19.

19. Alfred Jarry, cited in Graciela de Solá, *Proyecciones del surrealismo en la literatura argentina* (Buenos Aires: Ediciones Culturales Argentinas, 1967), p. 13.

20. Cortázar, cited in González Bermejo, *Cosas de escritores* (Montevideo:

Biblioteca de Marcha, 1971), p. 103.

21. André Breton, cited in M. Raymond, *De Baudelaire al surrealismo* (México: Fondo de Cultura Económica, 1960), p. 248.

22. Hatfield, p. 61.

23. Scalabrini, p. 125.

24. Wheelock, «The Subversive Borges,» *Texas Quarterly* 18, 1 (1975) 120.

25. See Wheelock, *The Mythmaker: A Study of Motif and Symbol in the Short Stories of Jorge Luis Borges* (Austin: University of Texas Press, 1969).

26. Scalabrini, p. 125.

27. Rodríguez Monegal, «Macedonio Fernández, Borges y el ultraísmo,» p. 178.

28. Marechal, cited in García's interviews, p. 73.

29. See Juan José Sebreli's discussion of Scalabrini's metamorphosis in the former's *Martínez Estrada, una rebelión inútil* (Buenos Aires: Jorge Alvarez, 1969), p. 33. Sebreli discusses the great fashion for intuitive social theories, pp. 31-35.

30. See Osvaldo Svanascini, *Xul Solar* (Buenos Aires: Ediciones Culturales Argentinas, 1962).

31. See Enrique Villegas, interview with García, p. 52.

32. Especially interesting in this respect is Culler's consideration of how readers are able to assimilate plot. For Culler, expectations built up through the experience of reading assist the reader in recuperating the matter of the plot from the new, strange form in which it appears in any new book. Maceodnio, then, makes use of these expectations to block the reader's attempts to make the work less strange and unknown. See Culler's discussion of plot in his above-cited book, pp. 205-24.

33. García, pp. 101-103.

34. García pp. 101-103.

35. Walter H. Sokel, *The Writer in Extremis: Expressionism in Twentieth-Century German Literature* (Stanford: Stanford University Press, 1959), p. 68.

36. Kayser, p. 193.

37. Frederick Brown, «Breton and the Surrealist Movement,» in John K. Simon, ed., *Modern French Criticism* (Chicago: University of Chicago Press, 1972), pp. 136-37.

38. Derrida, *L'Ecriture et al différence* (Paris: Seuil, 1967), p. 411. The original French reads as follows:

> le moment où le langage envahit le champ problématique universel; c'est alors le moment où, en l'absence de centre ou d'origine, tout devient discours--à condition de s'entendre sur ce mot--c'est-à-dire système dans lequel le signifié dentral, originaire ou transcendental, n'est jamais absolument présent hors d'un système de differences. L'absence de signifié transcendental étend a l'infini le champ et le jeu de la signification.

39.   Derrida, p. 410.

40.   Ana María Barrenechea, «Macedonio Fernández y su humorismo de la nada,» in Lafforgue's above-cited volume of essays, p. 75.

41.   Derrida, *Marges de la philosophie* (Paris: Editions de Minuit, 1962), p. 29.

42.   See Fernández Moreno's attempt to diagram this set of terms, p. 20; many terms appear to designate each category.

43.   These two points receive the most adequate discussion in Jitrik, *La novela futura de Macedonio Fernández.*

44.   Borinsky, «Macedonio: su proyecto novelístico,» p. 44, p. 47.

45.   Dellepiane, p. 59.

46.   See, for example, García's interviews with Marechal, p. 75, and with Francisco Luis Bernárdez, p. 91.

47.   García's interview with Peyrou, p. 81.

48.   The work in question is the title story in Augusto Roa Bastos, *Moriencia* (Caracas: Monte Avila, 1969). Foster's commentary appears in his «*La Pensée Sauvage* in A. Roa Bastos' Recent Fiction,» *Chasqui* 4, 2 (1975), 29-34.

49.   Cortázar, *Rayuela* (Buenos Aires: Sudamericana, 1963), p. 116.

50.   Ernesto Sábato comments on his novelistic characters in his essay, *El escritor y sus fantasmas* (Buenos Aires: Aguilar, 1963), p. 19.

51.   Cortázar, p. 428.

52.   Cortázar. p. 95.

53.   An instance of this type of criticism is Severo Sarduy's «Notas a las notas a las notas... A propósito de Manuel Puig,» *Revista Iberoamericana* 76-77 (1971), 555-67.

54.   Walter Kerr, «The New Theater is All Show,» *New York Times,* June 12, 1977, section 2, p. 5.

LITERARY CREATION AS PLAY

I.   A Stroll Through «Las espesuras de la nada»

A good deal of our discussion so far concerns Macedonio's endeavor to counter the harmful effects of modern-day civilization. A misdirected process of socialization has deformed readers of literature. They approach texts timidly, anxious for the author to provide them with order, reassuringly familiar literary devices and firm guidance. Reading Macedonio's writings ought to rid these readers of the need for authoritarian, pseudo-rationalistic art. These disheveled writings demand many sacrifices. Readers must learn to function in the absence of plot, believable characters, «trustworthy» language or narrative coherence. Nor can they expect a central, transcendental meaning to emerge from the text. The author announces the absence of any such meaning at the very outset.

At this point, one may justifiably ask what Macedonio does offer his readers in return for these sacrifices. What makes it worth-while to struggle with a text, knowing that it holds virtually none of the conventional comforts of literature? We have already seen one part of the answer in Macedonio's proposed reform of reading and writing. The author extends the opportunity to participate in the act of literary invention. Yet, the terms of this invitation may strike many as excessively Spartan. The innovator expects his readers to help create a «good» novel without knowing the specifications for such a work--for, indeed, none has ever existed before. Nor are the co-creators to be told the significance of the work. The absence of any pre-assigned significance is what provides the work with its center. These necessary conditions make the collaborators' task a most taxing one. Macedonio readily admits the considerable burden he imposes on his reading public with a literature «en la que se espera tanto... del lector, de su originalidad» (PR, p. 26).

Yet, Macedonio insists that the experience of making a «good» literature should be one of joy and pleasure. He is not being purely whimsical when he asserts that «no hay escrito mío en que no me acuerde al Fin de la comodidad del lector» (PR, p.34). The author describes his approach to literature by comparing it to easeful and liberating activities.

For example, the author's refusal to give a fixed meaning to his work appears as a way of sparing the reader: «no haré caer sobre usted ninguna hipótesis cruel» (PR, p. 21). The explorer of the new literature is likened to a man who, after years of laborious shaving with complicated paraphernalia, discovers he can do a much better job without putting himself through so much effort; conceptualization is much more agreeable and efficacious (PR, p. 80). Discarding the elaborate apparatus of conventional fiction is like discovering how to roast a lamb using only one candle and the force of imagination (PR, p. 80). The reader of the *Museo* must work out his own ending. Yet the author assures him that the open-ended novel is really much more easeful than the novel that ends conclusively (MNE, pp. 261-62). To end a novel forever, and without consulting the reader, is a harshly authoritative action: «Ningún autor tuvo la visión de la tortura del lector después de la palabra FIN» (MNE, p. 262).

In short, Macedonio's promise is that the new literature will be less burdensome to read than the conventional variety. While the reader of «bad» literature is subject to the domination of the author, the new reader can adapt the work to suit his own needs. The author who refrains from assigning a particular meaning to his work exhibits the same enjoyable dereliction as a man who deliberately sleeps through scholarly lectures (PR, p. 22). The reader confronted with a variety of possiblities enjoys the freedom of someone trying on new shoes; the author promises not to force him into making a decision (PR. p. 21). Over and over again, author and reader appear as joyous rule-breakers. They are pictured in images suggestive of liberation, playfulness, and the triumph over oppressive convention.

Thus it should be apparent that Macedonio's outlook on literature is essentially a cheerful one. There is no doubt that he shares many common concerns with other modern writers whose world view is an unhappy one. For instance, he is like the authors of the French theater of the absurd in rejecting language as an instrument of communication. However, the discovery that literature does not serve to communicate meaning is a liberating one in the Macedonian scheme. Unlike Beckett or Ionesco, the Argentine sees a host of new possibilities in language, once it has been freed from the burden of communication . The fact that a writer cannot succeed in transmitting a particular message to his readers is not an occasion for despair, but rather the point of departure for a literature rife with potential meanings.

To see what grounds Macedonio finds for such cheer, we should look again at the close correlation between his ideas and of those of Derrida. For Derrida, as for Macedonio, absence is not necessarily to be deplored. Macedonio is quick to point out the distinction between mere vacuity and a fruitful exploration of «la nada insolemne» (PR, p. 112). Having recognized the futility of trying to implant some lesson in his reader's mind, the truly aware author will base his further work on this insight. Rather than instruction, his writing will be an invitation to enjoy the absence of instruction: «Sería deplorable que el lector se extraviara en lo existente cuando yo le prometo como único arte pasearlo en las espesuras de la nada» (PR, p. 113). Here Macedonio emphasizes the link between absence and play. Because the author is no longer occupied with «la información o instructividad,» [1] he is free to play with language. The missing elements in his work are what allow the reader the free play of his imagination.

Absence and play appear correlated also in Derrida's vision of a culture that does not expect its language to be a sign system for the transmission of meaning:

> Thus language--and the sciences, ethnography in particular, it commands--emerges as a new center destined to replace the philosophic and/or epistemological center, or Origin, it has criticized and chased away. One myth cedes to another. The play *(jeu)* of signifiers, which Derrida calls a series of infinite substitutions, takes place on a field, or space, of language that is limited and marked by the lack of a center. Infinity is the result of a specific and finite absence. Play, which is another way of characterizing the totality of structures in language as they reflect each other, is supplementary to absence...Therefore play is the eternal disruption of the presence of a center (or Origin), in short, of presence itself, since the center identifies presence, but its lack signifies

absence. Derrida then goes on to distinguish two attitudes
toward absence. One is Rousseau's: negative, guilty, nostalgic.
The other is Nietzsche's: affirmative, joyous, forward-
looking...[2]

Said goes on to mention that Derrida sees little likelihood of
these affirmative attitudes taking hold in our present culture: «we
continue to be logocentric, and our minds remain rooted in a doctrine of signs, fastened upon the paradox of absence, committed to
difference rather than value. All we can do now is to catch a glimpse of the coming change in our outlook...»[3]

One easily recognizes here several key tenets of the Macedonian scheme of future culture. The Argentine envisions a writing
that will be «un órgano completamente puro por su perfecta in-
sipidez intrínseca»[4] once the central meaning has been purged. He
promises those who participate in this seemingly empty endeavor a
glimpse of infinity. The infinte possibilities for assembling a novel
out of the elements in the *Museo* can undo «Muerte Académica»
(MNE, p. 7), a condition of didactic, meaning-bound writings. The
reader who undertakes the making of the «good» novel can expect
an unlimited field for the exercise of his invention; the author
assures him that there will always be more for him to imagine
(MNE, p. 268). However, these promises of infinity only hold good
for those readers willing to make a genuine commitment of their
imaginative resources.

The problem for Macedonio, then, is to persuade his readers
to overcome their prejudice in favor of a solemn art based on solid
presences. Readers may be loath to accept an art based on uncer-
tainty, risk, daring and whimsy. The creator of this new art must
also be the one to provoke what Derrida sees as «the coming change
in our outlook,»[5] because that attitudinal change is the necessary
precondition for the exercise of his art. He must be not only the
practitioner of an artful playing with absences, but also the theorist
and evangelist of such activity. It is his task to make a game of infinite substitutions look like a worthwhile and fruitful artistic
undertaking.

The ways in which Macedonio invites his readers to play range
from forthright programmata to a deliberately shocking whim-
sicality to more covert structural and linguistic stratagems. His
first, most open tactic is to denounce solemnity in art and proclaim
the advent of playful literature. Seconding these pronouncements

are his whimsical literary practices. He entrusts the discussion of the most essential matters to a form of discourse bordering on nonsense. Esthetic and metaphysical questions become the subject matter of silly joking. Far from signaling disrespect for these ultimate questions, this witty, open-ended discourse conveys the author's resolve not to dictate his readers' beliefs. Ideally, the esthetic-metaphysical *capriccio* should possess a «fecundidad conciencial liberadora» (MNE, p. 266), freeing the reader to find his own truth. Thirdly, Macedonio plays with the rules we expect to find governing literary form and linguistic expression. Having shown both art and language to be unsuitable instruments for the communication of meaning, he demonstrates the alternative, less pragmatic, uses of both. Thus, working through both statements and artistic practice, he seeks to move literature toward the ideal of play.

II. An Esthetic of Game-Playing

Since Maceonio's esthetic of playfulness is so very unlike the conventional view of art, he sees a need to sketch it for the benefit of his readers. At the same time, the proposed new literature must appear to be something the reader can appreciate. Hence, Macedonio links the new, playful novel to reading experiences his readers already know, or reading experiences they secretly long for. Once more the innovator follows his policy of blaming the stagnation of literature neither on authors nor on readers, but on a generalized misconception of the literary enterprise.

An instance of this procedure is Macedonio's search for glimmers of the new «good» literature in the deficient literature of the past. In these literary judgments, high praise goes to those writers who incorporate elements of caprice and word-play into their writings. Disapproval greets those authors who try to force a particular message upon their readers or use an intimidatingly pompous tone. Both these criteria appear in the evaluation of Quevedo here summarized by Fernández Moreno: «Macedonio despreciaba una cosa en Quevedo: su moralismo; y admiraba dos: su humorismo y su pasión.»[6]

Despite his sweeping characterization of all past literature as bad, Macedonio is willing to recognize individual exceptions, «particularmente los chistes de Mark Twain» (PR, p. 93). Praising

Twain, the Argentine situates him as a precursor of twentieth-century vanguardist efforts, facetiously accusing the American of plagiarizing from him. The element of «good» literature to be found in Cervantes is also humorous in character.[7] Given Macedonio's orientation, it is not surprising to find him championing the work of Lawrence Sterne. The author of *Tristram Shandy* is a model of the literary comportment Macedonio values. His capricious humor, the disheveled structure of his writing, his continual toying with language and his avoidance of didacticism all commend him to anyone interested in the future of the novel. Macedonio uses Sterne as a point of reference in guiding his readers toward what is valuable in literature. At one point, for instance, he limits his literary pantheon to three figures: Mark Twain, Sterne and Gómez de la Serna (PR, pp. 25-26).

This last-named figure represents, for Macedonio, the best living example of the coming revolution in art: «el maestro único de la metáfora sin contexto, desideratum de la literatura que creo tomará todo el lugar de la puerilidad biográficoefusiva del poema construido, tentado de novelismo y del peor: el autonovelismo» (PR, p. 105). By leaving his work full of gaps and empty spaces, Gómez de la Serna succeeds in creating art without dominating it. Through his aberrant, humorous expression the Spaniard is able to «torturar todas las situaciones aparentes» (PR, p. 106) till they yield up their hidden reality. Thus Gómez de la Serna complies with the specifications of the new art: absence and play are everywhere evident in his work.

The existence of authors like Quevedo, Twain, Sterne and Gómez de la Serna, however, does not provide the only glimpse of this light-hearted literary future. Even when society officially insists that literary works be solemn and completely elaborated, readers secretly reject this misdirected esthetic. People inherently crave lightness and whimsy in writing, even if they have been trained to display reverence toward art. Macedonio appeals to his audience to choose between Wordsworth's revulsion with aerially copulating flies and an anonymous old woman's delighted «las moscas son alegría» (PR, p. 89). The instinctive reaction in favor of the buoyant attitude is to demonstrate the sound artistic intuitions of human beings: «¿Quién de ambos poseía más imaginación y poesía en el alma?» (PR, p. 89). The demand for moralizing, sententious art runs counter to the true feelings of the «público generoso, que tampoco consienta que en su espíritu ceda la piedad a lo artístico» (PR, p. 89). On the basis of this argument, Macedonio urges his audience to seek out the work of an artist who can suit its true needs, like Gómez de la Serna.

Even when schooling and the official literary climate favor reverent writings, Macedonio contends, readers secretly indulge their need for nonauthoritarian art. Macedonio offers himself as the exemplary delinquent reader. He disregards the most officially-sanctioned from of narration, history books. He not only sneers at them and fails to read them but disbelieves their «truths», contending that no history occurred before his own birth. The ponderous, sober approach to reality exemplified by history is unacceptable. Instead of being recorded, truth must be created by a suggestive, imaginative art, simultaneously «más gracioso y verdadero» (PR, p. 115).

Again and again Macedonio proclaims himself and everyone else to be in flagrant noncompliance with the norms of reverent readership. He points out that while many pay tribute to the writers of classical antiquity, none of us actually reads them. For instance, in a rumination on «el tema de la Literatura Obligatoria» (PR, pp. 149-50), the author admits to having read only one chapter of Homer. In his estimation, even Homer's Spanish translator really read no more than two chapters. The epic is unacceptable to Macedonio's esthetic because it is too completely narrated and bears too heavy a burden of charcterization and heroism. Although Macedonio admires the outstanding figures of Argentine literary history as men, he admits that their books can be very heavy going. Their journalistic writing, less self-consciously significant and more inclined to spontaneity, does give him esthetic satisfaction (PR, pp. 58-59). In another confession, the author describes his behavior while reading Anatole France: «he tratado de reírme, para no perder el ánimo, en los pasajes profundos» (PR, p. 180). While France's ability to provoke his readers to thought is commendable, Macedonio wishes that the Frenchman had not neglected the element of humor.

If readers do not read the solemn, «important» works they are taught to admire, that does not mean they go without literature. While apparently acquiescing to the official attitude of quasi-religious respect for art, they may covertly play games with it. An example of this healthy delinquency is a lecture audience savoring the spectacle of a famous author «que se palpa de existencia escuchándose en público» (PR, p. 294). Macedonio finds the

Argentine public especially skilled at this type of clandestine ir-
reverence. Such gameplaying should become the preferred model
of literary comportment, not only for audiences but for lecturing
authors. All parties in such a literary transaction should act in a
shamelessly facetious spirit. The innovator designates such caprice
as «la cachada» and proclaims it the remedy for «la conferenciabilidad» (PR, pp. 294-95), sobriety about authors and writing.
In short, readers are deeply disaffected from the joyless ideal of
literature imposed by the general culture and forever devising new
ways to circumvent it.

The natural inclination to play manifests itself despite society's
attempts to stifle it. What Macedonio proposes is to make this
aberrant tendency into an esthetic principle. Works like *Tristram
Shandy* and behavior like that of the irreverent lecture-goers show
that people crave and appreciate a gamelike approach to literature.
Now, whimsy and silliness should be granted legitimacy as components of artistic expression. We should acknowledge that art is
kept alive by «grandes ocasiones payasescas» (PR, p. 295), by «in-
solencia» (PR, p. 112) and by «la nada insolemne» (PR, p. 112).
The element of literature we tend to overlook should now receive its
due: the «alusión a la felicidad» that gives readers so much of their
reading pleasure and literature so much of its power. Therefore,
Macedonio sets out to create a literature that constantly draws attention to «la condición hedónica fundamental, sin la cual ese
placer no se produce».[*] Comicity should not be a lure to attract
readers to the text, but rather the *fontis ab qua* that work's artistic
efficacy flows.

III.   Playful Treatment of Crucial Matters

If humor receives such a high place in Macedonio's announced hierarchy of values, then he should be willing to employ
humorous discourse to treat the most important matters. This procedure represents a break with an attitude widespread in
Macedonio's environment but meaningless to him: that one should
not joke when life-and-death matters are under discussion. Rejecting the distinction between silliness and seriousness, he entrusts his
most crucial themes to a wildly capricious form of expression. The
Museo, a work of great whimsy, is the repository of the author's
most important thoughts on existence, death, imagination,

esthetics and other far-from-trivial matters. By allowing his themes to reach the reader by means of jokes and puzzles, Macedonio proves his faith in the superiority of play over pontification.

For instance, as we have seen, Macedonio's esthetic scheme demands the incorporation of productive absences into the literary work. We know his opposition to the completely elaborated text was genuine. Yet he exploits the comic possibilities inherent in the notion of being the author of silences. An outraged «internal reader» of the *Museo* accuses the author of «ahorrar trama» (MNE, p. 252) once his writerly-imaginative resources have been depleted. This reader claims that the author of absences is really a shirker who prefers to let his characters and readers do all the work for him. Even though this disgruntled individual retracts his accusations under pressure from the other readers, he has still pointed out the most ludicrous aspects of Macedonian vanguardism.

Moreover, the author himself points out the resemblance between his purposeful use of absence and mere sloth or ineptitude. In «El no-hacer» he develops his theory of absences by means of an analogy of a burlesque sort. He describes a ranch whose entire staff devotes itself to programmatic sloth. This ludicrous scenario, seconded by a further analogy with the listlessness of civil servants, makes the literary exploration of silence seem like a very funny proposition. At the same time, this funny proposition is a major tenet in the program of the very man who is making sport of it (PR, pp. 138-41).

Along with laziness, lack of skill is offered as an explanation for the author's deviant practices. This idea is a familiar one among opponents of experimentation in art. As is well known, reactionary critics are fond of comparing the vanguardist's efforts unfavorably to the drawings of young children or other untrained artists. They suggest the innovator is proclaiming his lack of technical mastery a virtue. Macedonio uses this rather tiresome joke as an abrasive from of irony directed against the bourgeois concept of «awe-inspiring» art. In his scheme, nothing is more repressive than an author who intimidates his readers with a dazzling display of technical expertise. Rather than demonstrate he can do something the readers cannot, the author should emphasize that all are partners in the labor of creation. While the reading of a partially deconstructed novel may be arduous, readers should remember that the author has trusted their ability to accomplish this creative task. His confidence in his readers makes him superior to a master craftsman who offers readers the «descortesía» of a «libro vacío y perfecto» (MNE, p. 14). For Macedonio to employ such irony implies a special risk. Even if readers do not take his self-deprecations literally, they may still come to regard him as no more than an eccentric humorist. As Lafforgue[9] and Jitrik[10] point out, the image of the innovator as purely a jester has been common among even some of his greatest admirers.

An instance of this risk-taking irony is Macedonio's exposition of his plan for literary incompleteness. Derrida, working with the same ideas, speaks of the critic's «deconstruction»[11] of a text. The Argentine refers, less augustly, to the author-critic's «frangollo» (MNE, p. 14). His analogies for the deconstruction of the text are not lofty ones. For instance, in «Aquí es el boliche remendón de 'La perfecta descompostura,'» (PR, pp. 166-67) the author describes a workshop whose master craftsman finally realizes the futility of trying to restore objects to perfection. After years of painstaking efforts to halt the work of entropy, he is able to recognize disintegration and decomposition as natural parts of existence. Continual reinvention, rather than reworking of the same aging objets, becomes his new goal. The illuminated repairman abandons his obsessive labors and kills himself in order to be reincarnated in a fresh body. This silly fable contains several key Macedonian tenets concerning originality, the fallacy of polished art and the natural wisdom of biological processes.

The element of risk is greater yet when Macedonio makes a game of the entire literary transaction. Like Derrida, Macedonio notes the reactionary author's tendency to use written language, potentially an adventurous medium, to minimize risk and spontaneity in art.[12] The attempt to monumentalize language into fixed, immutable works of literature is antiartistic. García's book of interviews documents some of Macedonio's deliberately perishable literary endeavors, designed to last no longer than their elaboration. One discussant recalls Macedonio taking him and Borges to a shack in a vacant lot to engage in a discussion of poetics and metaphysics.[13] Another describes the innovator's practice of entertaining youthful admirers while hidden behind a curtain--as García points out, a behavioral extension of the esthetic doctrine of absences.[14] Other episodes suggest that Macedonio was a practitioner of what later would come to be designated as happenings, *fluxus,* total theater or process art: transitory art works that do not seek to fossilize or monumentalize themselves. Such «throw-away» literary actions have no existence today except as recollected by participants from the *Martín Fierro* group.

Beyond their anecdotal value, however, the spontaneous Macedonian projects express a social ideal especially current among innovative thinkers of the twentieth century: that of the playful society. Champions of this utopian scheme include Johann Huizinga in his 1955 *Homo Ludens: A Study of the Play-Element in Culture,* Norman O. Brown, writing in 1957 *(Love's Body),* Herbert Marcuse in the 1955 *Eros and Civilization* and Harvey Cox, whose *The Feast of Fools* appeared in 1972. From different perspectives, these men all proclaim playfulness to be a social virtue much neglected in recent years.

Huizinga, for instance, sees in the history of Western culture a continuous degradation of the value of non-goal-directed activity. In his analysis, society has misplaced its values by assigning importance only to those endeavors whose end product has some recognized utility. Thus the playful sphere of human activity is relegated to the status of time-killing. His recommendation is that mankind accord recognition to the humanizing effect of activities without any material objective. For him, a truly integrated culture must allow its citizens to feel they are doing something dignified and profoundly human when they engage in play.

The same critique of present society is present in Marcuse's work, but his utopian vision makes him even more closely related to Macedonio. In Marcuse's program, the first feature specified for the ideal society is «The transformation of toil (labor) into play, and of repressive productivity into 'display'--a transformation that must be preceded by the conquest of want (scarcity) as the determining factor of civilization.»[15] Indeed, he emphasizes that no culture can be nonrepressive in character until it encourages the cultivation of man's capacity for «useless» invention: «We recall the constitutive role attributed to imagination (phantasy) in play and display. Imagination preserves the objectives of those mental processes which have remained free from the repressive reality principle; in their esthetic function, they can be incorporated into the conscious rationality of mature civilization. The play impulse stands for the common denominator of the two opposed mental processes and principles.»[16]

Marcuse comes very close to Macedonio in his intense concern that the human imaginative faculties not be subjected to restrictions: «Play and display, as principles of civilization, imply not the transformation of labor but its complete subordination to the freely evolving potentialities of man and nature.»[17] Here we see a reflection of Macedonio's insistence that authors must learn to give freedom to their characters and to their readers lest imagination and fantasy atrophy. Part of what people do, Macedonio tells us, must always be left free of any predetermined goal: metaphysical speculation and art fulfill this need especially well.

Chance, daring and risk-taking, important in gameplaying, figure prominently in Macedonio's writings. One text is entitled «Boletería de la gratuidad» (pp. 37-39); another furnishes an «Ejemplo de la literatura de circunstancias» (pp. 128-29). In his persona of «El Bobo de Buenos Aires,» Macedonio plays a holy fool untainted by the pragmatic notions of art that plague the city's literary establishment. His clowning reveals how art may satisfy man's need for activity without immediate usefulness.

IV.   Language Games

Language becomes a prime material for this jesting. Accepting the conventions of language is implicitly supportive of the esthetic *status quo.* Only by taking the linguistic mechanism apart can an author transform his writing into what Derrida calls «a game of pure risk.»[18]

Macedonio illustrates this new questioning spirit with a visit to the workshop run by Xul Solar, «Idiomas en compostura» (MNE, p. 47.» To create a formulaic art, he needs words with no existence outside the work of fiction in which they occur. Xul Solar helps him fit together a number of compound adjectives out of constituent elements already extant in real-world Spanish. Xul's activity involves a Spanish pun, since *compostura,* his specialty, can mean *compounding* as well as *repairing.* Both meanings apply here, since Macedonio really is retooling Spanish to make it more suitable for expressionist writing. Since even compound nouns are quite rare in Spanish the creation of compound adjectives represents a further departure from what exists in real-world language.

Macedonio's first new creations are intelligible adjectives obviously patterned on German syntax, e.g., «Al 'por-todos-nosotros-artistas-servido-de-ensueños' Lector.» Here one could suspect Macedonio of seeking to augment the expressive capacities of Spanish. While he was writing the *Museo,* his friend Borges was proselytizing for the «de-rhetoricizing» of Spanish. Borges preached the need for more compression, and frequently held up the Germanic languages, with their compounds, as models. However, as one progresses through Macedonio's forms, it becomes increasingly clear that chaos, not elegant communication, is his goal. The final entry in his list reads: «A 'lo-menos-real, el-que-sueña-sueños-de-otro, -y-más fuerte-en-realidad, -pues-no-la pierde-aunque-no-lo-dejan-soñar-sino-sólo-resoñar' Lector.» This tormented form is tantamount to an admission that the entire episode has been a pretext for playing extravagant games with language. Macedonio frequently plants such admissions amid his confusing texts to remind readers of the great ludic element in his verbal experimentation.

Macedonio's linguistic jokes rely on two basic types of strategy. One is a mimicry of the unwieldiness language can exhibit on the tongues and in the hands of competent speakers. These oddities are recognizably akin to the expression of a Spanish speaker who is inattentive, overexcited, berserk or burdened by a stiff, laborious rhetoric. A second type of joking involves the creation of aberrant utterances unlike what might be produced by a competent speaker of Spanish or, indeed, of human language. These strange verbal formulae are at odds with the way man perceives and organizes experience. The first type of humor amuses by striking a familiar note, while the second is funny because it is so very unrecognizable.

To this first type of humor belongs the most noted aspect of Macedonio's linguistic gamesmanship, his neologisms. Many of his coinings follow the accepted Spanish pattern for the formation of nouns from existing adjectives, e.g., *instructividad* from *instructivo*. Others are feigned noun forms derived from verbs that occur in real-world Spanish, such as *conferenciabilidad* from *conferenciar*. These neologisms have the feature of instant recognizability because they conform to the rules by which Spanish allows new nouns to occur, i.e., they represent so-called «lexical gaps» that are potentially fillable. The reader is continually encountering words that seem right and make sense, although they have no currency outside the Macedonian lexicon. What is funny, though, is the light-hearted author's mimicry of a pompous treatise-writer trying to daunt his readers with an overabundance of syllables. Fernández Moreno likens these feigned words to the terminology of phrenological texts. Macedonio, inventor of an open, nonreppresive discourse, makes ironic use of the reactionary author's tactics.

Papeles abounds in mockeries of the cumbersome rhetorical style found in so much «official» Spanish. One instance of this «nueva Oficiosidad» presents the virtually complete fossilization of discourse. A pedant swathes an inane datum in periphrastic and highly conventional verbal formulae:

> --Señor: vengo, sabedor de la manifestación de usted de no sospechar cómo se le ocurrió la feliz idea musical realizada en el existoso tango 'Siempre más', a expresarle que yo lo sé, de manera que tendré el placer de alegrarlo poniendo término a su duda, porque comprendo que un autor original no está cómodo mientras no consigue saber de dónde le vino o qué le estimuló, una concepción artística. Su tango, señor, está muy aproximadamente dado en la música norteamericana del film parlante 'Abajo el Telón' (PR, p. 146).

Macedonio makes special use of the type of syntactic and stylistic errors a fairly competent speaker may make in the actual performance of speech or writing. For instance, he invents for himself an overeffusive admirer. The admirer commits a gross redundancy in his eagerness to praise the master: «Hasta hoy no había leído ninguna de sus obras. Me refiero a sus obras escritas.» His rhetorical attempts to juxtapose his unworthy existence with Macedonio's original mode of living also fail. An effort at self-denigration turns into ridiculous contradiction: «me empeñaba en no malograr mis fracasos.» Trying to formulate an appropriately hyperbolic expression of his hero's natural gifts, the admirer loses his common sense and writes: «Macedonio Fernández no nació desnudo» (PR, p. 123).

The excitability of the admirer is only part of his expressive problem. He also commits infelicities while trying to achieve a «poetic» formulation of his devotion. A deliberately deviant mixing of realia and abstractions turns out to be jarring rather than lyrical: «De un lado de la pared, su cuarto, denso del humo de mil marcas de cigarrillos, de ideas y de sentires» (PR, p. 123). A pseudo-innovative desire to «foreground» language leads the devotee to write these idiotic fragments: «Tango del pensar. Cigarrillos del pensar. Cuarto desnudo del pensar. Desorden del pensar. Rasgueo del pensar» (PR, p. 123). After committing all these offenses in the pursuit of a highly poetic language, the admirer displays a startling lack of insight into his own linguistic procedures. He concludes his letter by congratulating himself for using *quiero* rather than the loftier *deseo* to express his longing to be with his idol. This choice of words supposedly gives his writing «ropas de trabajo» (PR, p. 124) instead of the fancy dress of a self-consciously literary linguistic standard.

The entire letter (PR, pp. 123-24) becomes a horrible example of poetically distorted language ill-used by someone who does not understand its purposes and is too overwrought to express himself in any mode. The less talented of the youthful vanguardists who championed Macedonio must have afforded many models of such faulty expression.

A second type of amusement comes from statements no real person, however excited or pseudopoetic, would make. Many times, the speaker will produce a grammatically well-formed sentence, but reveal a curious ignorance of how the real world functions. This is the problem of the passerby who says «--Señor, vea que se moja el paraguas» (PR, p. 146). The Buenos Aires Boob is given to telling people on the street: «le aviso que la punta de ese cigarillo se le está quemando» (PR, p. 147).

An extreme instance of this type of humor occurs in «Una novela para nervios sólidos» (PR, pp. 167-68). Here the narrator is correct in his syntax, but displays disregard for the real attributes of the objects that figure in the story:

> ... le retiré la percha al sombrero y en las mangas de éste introduje ambos brazos, di cuerda al almanaque, arranqué la hojita del día al reloj y eché carbón a la heladera, aumenté hielo a la estufa, añadí al termómetro colgado todos los termómetros que tenía guardados para combatir el frío que empezaba, y como pasaba alcanzablemente un lento tranvía di el salto hacia la vereda y caí cómodamente sentado en mi buen sillón de escritorio (PR, p. 167).

Here Macedonio is not just creating chaos but also fulfilling one of his own literary demands: to find a form of expression that is not continually referring to the real world. As the expressionist esthetic specifies, he undertakes «the search for an original artistic version of /phenomena/: thence a form of literature which refuses to be only a document...»[19] The above-quoted «novel» breaks off all ties to the world of our experience. Literature is a realm where calendars may have the feature of windability, thermometers have anti-cold properties and hats may be classified among the sleeved garments.

A series of playful autobiographies situates Macedonio's life in this realm alien to our real-world experience. For instance, this world confuses learned behaviors and spontaneous actions requiring no coaching: «A los siete anos ya aprendí a venirme abajo de un balcón y llorar en seguida» (PR, p. 119). This type of humor appears, years later, in the writings of **Macedonio's** self-professed admirer, Julio Cortázar.[20] Cortázar's 1966 *Historias de cronopios y famas* contains detailed instructions for crying, bursting into song and other unpremeditated actions. Whether or not any direct influence exists, the resemblance shows how Macedonio, like the *nueva narrativa,* wrests language away from our conventional organization of real-world experience.

For example, we accept that a person or other animal is born in a literal sense. One may also speak of the birth of something inanimate or abstract, using a figure of speech. Macedonio, though, indiscriminately throws together animate and inanimate, literal and figurative, to produce a startling statement of solipcism: «El Universo o Realidad y yo nacimos el 1º de junio de 1874» (PR, p. 115). The vast, abstract birth and the actual one are both reported as taking place «cerca de aquí y en una ciudad de Buenos Aires» (PR, p. 115). The solipcist's main point, which he subsequently argues, is that there is no absolute reality «out there.» Rather, «la Realidad que hay la traemos nosotros» (PR, p. 115). The philosophical argument may not be brilliantly original, but the method of argumentation is. Before he even presents his idea, the author has already assaulted the notion of an absolute reality with the linguistic deviance of his opening sentence. Because the concept of reality receives too solemn a treatment in the real world, in Macedonio's writings it is disrespectfully stripped of its awesomely abstract quality.

Indeed, the author thinks all the great metaphysical conceptions command too much official respect. To show metaphysics as a field for invention and play, he makes its abstract concepts perform actions that only a much lowlier agent can properly carry out. In one story, for instance, the Cosmos fights an overgrown squash from the north of Argentina--and loses. At the end, the triumphant squash is planning to take on «la Creación... la Vía Láctea... el Ser, la Realidad y su Cáscara» (PR, p. 163).

Apart from the events of the plot, this story amuses by the un-dignified linguistic treatment it gives to the lofty terminology of metaphysicians. The soul of a cell is heard conspiring to itself: «yo quiero apoderarme de todo el 'stock', de toda la 'existencia en plaza' de Materia» (PR, p. 162). After subjecting cosmology to such trivialization, the author suggests everyone take a more open approach to these matters: «dada la relatividad de las magnitudes todas, nadie de nosotros sabrá si vive o no dentro de un zapallo» (PR, p. 162).

Startling, too, are the Macedonian characters who put language to uses no real person would be liable to devise for it. Among these is an individual who, boundlessly confident of the power of language to communicate meaning, informs his dog in detail about the visit of a guest. When the detailed explanation fails to persuade the dog not to bite the visitor, the owner does not ques-tion the efficacy of using speech to control his dog's behavior. Rather, he blames himself for having phrased his message poorly and offers a reworked version (PR, p. 168). The surprise and humor here come from the owner's curious conviction that speech can be perfected as an instrument of inter-species communication. Yet, in a sense, this notion is only an extension of the widespread delusion that linguistic expression can be fashioned into a flawless transmitter of messages.

Another communication-crazed individual sends Macedonio an enthusiastically-written biography of the latter. Since the biographer is someone who has been completely out of touch with his subject for ten years, this communication causes more shock than pleasure. The recipient of the biography-by-mail devises a meaning for the whole event. He offers it as a notable datum about himself to be used by any reader who might care to make a biographical statement about him (PR, p. 122).

The convention that language must sometimes be used to cover up certain untoward situations seems to have escaped another character. He is heard to say: «Estoy esperando que alguna vez no todos los componentes del Jurado Municipal y del Nacional de premios a la producción literaria sean amigos míos, para presen-tarme al concurso» (PR, p. 146). This speaker is aberrant, not for his faith in the possiblity of communication, but for his faith in its desirability.

The complicated rules governing thank-you notes, apologies,

congratulations, introductions and other conventional transactions are another source of Macedonian humor, El Bobo de Buenos Aires has a particularly poor mastery of these matters. On one occasion, he writes to every house in Buenos Aires, congratulating the occupant for not living in the house falsely reported as having burned that day. However, he does not know the address of the house in the report, and has to add an apology to the congratulation in case the recipient of the letter is the victim of the reported fire.

Sociolinguistic deviance creates a bizarre scene in «Vivir disculpando» (PR, pp. 157-58). Here a group of five normal speakers is invaded by a man who apologizes aggressively to them for his existence. The normal individuals try to bring the conversation back within the rules by extending their forgiveness and offering to introduce the invader. He continues to produce confusion and rupture: «Muy bien, pero presentadme las edades de cada uno, no los nombres» (PR, p. 157). The deviant subjects his listeners to a scathing critique of the customs governing behavior in social situations and leaves two of them with sympathy cards because he will not be alive to attend their funerals. The author steps in to reassure the reader that he does not approve of this type of linguistic aberrance, which only serves to «hacerse desagradable a los demás» (PR, p. 158).

Macedonio's inventions include a number of paeans, formal apologies, condolences and expressions of gratitude designed for use in peculiar situations. These mimic the code of their real-world model only to show up their essential silliness. Among these are an apology for ugly men to use upon being introduced to a lady (PR, p. 153), an excuse for those who are unable to attend a banquet but able to send a substitute (PR, pp. 71-72) and a method for praising nonexistent things (PR, pp. 112-14). Confronting the question of how long a toastmaster should speak, he invents the «brindis sin fin» (PR, p. 68). A variant of this invention is bringing the endless toast to an end, a maneuver whose result is total silence (PR, p. 69). In his «Lo que sólo deben saber quienes esto escuchen» (PR, pp. 85-89), he claims to invent a form of public discourse composed entirely of secrets.

Types of verbal interaction requiring the mastery of complicated formulae have a double function for Macedonio. On the one hand, he «straightforwardly» uses toasts to bestow praise, letters to express friendship and speechmaking to propound his reforms. At the same time, his apparent compliance with the rules of toastmaking, correspondence and oratory can suddenly change to anarchic disruption. A letter to Jorge Luis Borges is an apology for missing an arranged meeting and the setting-up of a future visit. Both points are communicated, but the rest of the letter is an accumulation of bizarre aberrations. The set phrase «si no hay inconveniente» becomes, nonsensically, «si hay inconveniente» (PR, p. 90). The writer seems unable to maintain consistency in his announced mesage or in its verbal formulation. The first sentence informs the recipient that Macedonio will stay for supper «si hay inconveniente y estamos con ganas de trabajar». The *si* construction makes feeling like working a necessary precondition to staying to supper. Macedonio's commentary on his original statement, though, makes staying for supper a more probable occurrence than feeling like working: «Advertirás que las ganas de cenar las tengo aun con inconveniente y sólo falta asegurarme las otras» (PR, p. 90).

Inconsistency of verb forms also produces confusion as Macedonio abruptly switches to the present tense and back again: «Soy tan distraído que iba para allá y en el camino me acuerdo de que me había quedado en casa» (PR, p. 90). This syntactic oddity appears to have no expressive function other than that of disorienting the reader.

A lack of coordination between what the author claims he is doing and his actual practices becomes patent in mid-letter. Having dispatched the main business of the letter, the apology and re-invitation, the author suddenly announces: «Su objeto es...» (PR, p. 90) and launches into a nonsensical and unrelated story. Here again the careful compliance with letter-writer's etiquette is jarring. The self-consciously civilized phraseology makes more patent the disorder that manifests itself at the semantic and syntactic levels and in the increasingly fantastic events the letter relates.

A diffuse joke emerges from the small aberrations in the verbal texture of all Macedonian writings. These randomly-occurring oddities move Macedonian expression farther away from real-world speech and writing and heighten the reader's confusion. For instance, the sentence «Fueron tantos los que faltaron que si falta uno más no cabe» (PR, p. 153) has won much attention for its spectacular logical flaw. A second form of deviance, though, appears in the inconsistency of the verb forms. The reader feels that something has changed between the second and third clauses to shift the time frame into the present, but he has missed it. Orthographic inconsistencies also create this unnerving effect. Capitalization seems to follow no rules as Macedonio refers to «el Lector de Tapa, Lector de Puerta-Lector Mínimo, o Lector No-conseguido» and then to the «Lector-mínimo» (MNE, p. 83). This unruliness makes the text unbearable for a reader who believes in the strict and standard enforcement of rules. To persevere, one must accept Macedonio's premise that linguistic expression is an anarchic sport.

V.   A Festive Utopia

Macedonio's linguistic joking is indicative of his anarchistic spirit of play. Any type of rule-governed behavior is inherently funny and invites the inventive soul to commit infractions. Language is the most immediate variety of rule-governed behavior and one in which writers are conventionally allowed to exercise their «poetic license.» Macedonio takes advantage of this situation to barrage his readers with all manner of gross and subtle deviations from the norm.

Even the most capricious of these aberrations, however, forms part of a larger scheme. Because language is key to our organization and interpretation of experience, the author seeks to make his unruly language a truly subversive expression. If the reader sees the towering metaphysical concepts treated with linguistic disrespect, he may come to adopt a more playful attitude toward them. If he sees the author's willful violation of rules as a pleasurable activity, he may lose his own fear of authority. Macedonio shows the reader that literature can be liberated from the «serious» mission of producing masterworks and language from the task of communicating meaning, yet literature and language can still be worthwhile play activities.

Although Macedonio's gameplaying occurs in the realms of language, art and metaphysical speculation, he means to contaminate all of human existence with elements of sport, risk-taking and chance. This goal is manifest in such programmatic writings as the «Editorial de Regreso de la 'Revista Oral' de Córdoba» (PR, pp. 52-55). Here the author lists his two great obsessions: to establish the validity of «mystical» thought and to minimize the restrictions society places upon its members. Macedonio's literary playfulness and unruliness offer a model for human behavior in a nonrepressive, festive utopia.

NOTES

1. Fernández, cited in Fernández Moreno, p. 16.
2. Edward W. Said, «Abecedarium Culture,» in John Simon, ed., *Modern French Criticism* (Chicago: University of Chicago press, 1972), pp. 383-84.
3. *Ibid.*
4. Fernández, cited in Fernández Moreno, p. 17.
5. Said, p. 384, summarizes Derrida's concept.
6. Fernández Moreno, p. 17.
7. See Fernández Moreno's discussion, p. 18.
8. Fernández, cited in Fernández Moreno, p. 19.
9. Lafforgue, p. 17.
10. Jitrik, p. 158.
11. For instance, Derrida uses this term and the concept it represents in his *De la grammatologie* (Paris: Editions de Minuit, 1967), p. 39.
12. Derrida complains that the reactionary writer uses writing to monumentalize what he says, but yet sees written language as potentially more full of risk and play in the hands of an audacious writer; a key point in *L'Ecriture et la différence.*
13. *García's interview with Bernárdez,* p. 87.
14. *García's interview with Pedrido,* p. 40. García's comment on the matter, p. 119.
15. Herbert Marcuse, *Eros and Civilization* (Boston: Beacon, 1955), p. 193.
16. *Ibid.*
17. Marcuse, p. 195.
18. Derrida's precept is here summarized by Said, p. 385.
19. Foster, *Unamuno and the Novel as Expressionistic Conceit,* p. 8.
20. See Cortázar's discussion of Macedonio's humor in his interview with González Bermúdez in the latter's *Cosas de escritores* (Montevideo: Biblioteca de Marcha, 1971), p. 102.

RETROSPECTIVE APPRAISAL

I. An Author with an Eye to the Future

Macedonio makes it clear that we are not to judge his labors by their visible results. To begin with, he values inventive process over artistic product. If successful, his work should invite re-elaboration and resist completion. Moreover, he attempts artistic feats beyond the capacity of contemporary man, including himself. For instance, his forward-looking esthetic calls for writing to be centered on silence. Yet, as he points out, the rhetoric of silence is only being developed (PR, p. 65). Although Macedonio cannot see the realization of his own goals, he offers a model and a prophecy for the future. He presents himself not as a master craftsman, but as an innovator and seer. Half a century after Macedonio launched his experiment, it is fair to ask how workable his inventions, and how accurate his prophecies, have proven themselves.

As we have seen, Macedonio's work proposes a multiplicity of ways for mankind to save itself from intellectual and spiritual stagnation. Some of his suggestions enjoyed a degree of currency in their historical moment, but lost much of their appeal in subsequent years. Such is the case of the Macedonian plan to turn philosophy into a province of irrational discourse. Analytic philosophy, far from capitulating to intuitive metaphysics, continues to aspire to the rigor of an exact science. Intuitive works such as *No toda es vigilia* and the *Geisteswissenschaft* studies in the German university system caused excitement upon publication, but have since become museum pieces. Here Macedonio showed himself to be very much a man of his time, the expressionistic *entreguerre* period, but a poor prophet as yet.

Other of Macedonio's projects are still too radical for us. Today more readers are willing to experience a literature of fragments and absences. Yet, the exhortation to «read» a novel without support from a written text is as daunting as ever. Despite Macedonio's proclamation of reader liberation, readers continue to look to authors for guidance and control. The freedom to edit or emend an author's work is alien to us. We feel the need for a definitive text «as the author intended.» In these respects, the Macedonian utopia of reader competence has not become a reality. Of course, the innovator did not specify when the liberated consciousness of readers would emerge. It is possible that a future generation of readers, less inhibited and less dependent on words than ourselves, will carry out Macedonio's blueprint for the unwritten novel. Writing in 1967, Derrida finds Western civilization to have made little progress in overcoming its logocentrism. He, too, posits the likelihood of an attitudinal change in the future resulting in greater acceptance of artistic silence.[1]

Other of Macedonio's prophecies have seen partial fulfillment. His belief that future authors would no longer allow their presence and opinions to dominate their works is in this category. One of the factors differentiating the *nueva narrativa* from Macedonio's novelistic ideal is the former's insistence that imaginative literature can also serve as social commentary. At the same time, though, today's author does permit his readers to assume a more active role in the formulation of that commentary.

II.   Limited Fulfillment of Macedonio's Prophecies

An instance of a modern author who approaches Macedonio's goal might be Severo Sarduy, the Cuban-French author and theorist. Sarduy's lack of interest in establishing any very direct communication with his readers became especially evident with the publication of his 1972 *Cobra*. In this novel, the apparent subject matter is largely inane. The events of the plot consist of the transformations of a character who is, at various moments, female, male, large, small, normally-proportioned and deformed. The *raison d'être* of the work clearly lies elsewhere, in its linguistic experimentation and its implementation of certain new ideas about the structure of literary work.

Sarduy, however, is much further removed from direct communication with his readers than are most creators of the *nueva narrativa*. Yet even Sarduy's works contain a form of commentary on social realities of a fairly specific nature. Critics have studied the Cuban's writings as a reflection of Cuban history and social structure.[2]

More typical of the *nueva narrativa* is the continual reference to real-world conditions. The fiction of the Colombian Gabriel García Márquez, for instance, complies with Macedonio's demands for irrationalism, imagination and nonlinear structure. Yet the effect is not, as the earlier innovator hoped, to prevent language from speaking (PR, p. 310). Iris Josefina Ludmer has shown that the Colombian's formal innovations serve to structure meaning and hence to provide readers with access to that meaning.[3] The so-called «magical» representation is an effective way of communicating Third World realities.[4] True, Macedonio's demand that art deny meaning is equivocal and coexists with an insistence on art's significance. Yet he cannot be seen as endorsing the *nueva narrativa's* use of irrationalism and foregrounded language to comment on political and economic conditions.[5]

Where Macedonio most exemplifies the tendencies of his age is in the spirit of radical self-questioning that pervades his work. Literature, metaphysics, cultural and social criticism all require the continual reexamination of their basic principles and practices. The metaphysician, for instance, is free to invent a new method of philosophical inquiry. Macedonio gives the model for reinventing philosophy and encourages his readers to make the experiment themselves (PR, pp. 162-63). However, implicit in this new liberty is a new task. Each discussant must choose what aspects of reality merit scrutiny and how that inquiry should proceed. Participation in longstanding metaphysical debates using well-established methodologies is not an option Macedonio will recognize.

III. Self-Questioning Texts

Critics of Macedonio's literary production have noted how much attention it calls to its own mechanisms. For García, the notable feature of the *Museo* is «que la escritura de la novela se convierte en tema principal de la novela.»[6] Jitrik, too, finds the foregrounding of the process of writing key to the Macedonian innovative effort. In his listing of the principle features of Macedonio's «good» novel, the second is: «Ningún 'texto' puede excluir su proceso de constitución, no mostrar en sí mismo, en su misma forma, cómo se produce.»[7] The reader is made privy to the workings of literary creation so that he may consider for himself what they ought to be and how he may contribute to them.

The most obvious sign of this process of self-questioning is the number of interrogative sentences found throughout Macedonio's work. Moreover, these are not principally rhetorical questions whose answer is near at hand. The author disdains the practice of posing problems that can easily be resolved (PR, p. 42). His own questions imply a ceaseless reconsideration of the activities of reading and writing. In the midst of a text, he stops to wonder: «Alargar ¿es genial o no es genial?» (PR, p. 194). After ruminating on how many of his thoughts will already have occurred to readers, he asks: «¿Para quién habré escrito yo todo esto...?» (PR, p. 240). These troubling questions preclude a reading based purely on acquired habits. The premises of literary action are permanently in the foreground and subject to review.

Self-interrogation does not end with the specific literary transaction between Macedonio and his reader. Many more questions arise, questions concerning every enterprise in art, language and communication. For instance, the author proposes: «Al que se dice artista podemos preguntarle siempre: ¿Cómo ha intentado usted la Tragedia?» (PR, pp. 283-84). No artist is entitled to evade this problem.

The reader finds a number of questions touching on aspects of literary creation he would, perhaps, prefer not to consider. For instance, Macedonio wonders why it is that so many of the great men of Argentine literature produced such dull writings (PR, p. 59). In his toast to Marinetti, he openly asks how the inventor of such a liberating esthetic can also be the proponent of such a reactionary political program (pp. 72-75). Such behavior, unorthodox in a toastmaster, does not seek to offend; indeed, Macedonio is quick to praise Marinetti's pioneering art. Rather, it is a way of forcing all present to consider a persistent and baffling literary conundrum. The Macedonian toast is often a self-doubting form of discourse. Concluding his remarks, the toastmaster wonders whether anything he can say will communicate the virtues of the toast's object. In toasts to Marechal (PR, pp. 75-77) and Scalabrini Ortiz (PR, pp. 79-82), he largely abandons the attempt to tell the audience why he admires these men, opting instead to speak of other matters. A letter to Pedro Juan Vignale points out the oddity of writing to an absent friend as if no break in habitual face-to-face interaction had occurred. Rejecting the conventional fiction, the letter-writer draws attention to the attenuated contact between himself and the recipient: «Qué precioso *era* Pedro Juan Vignale» (PR, p. 108).

In each case, the author forces our attention to one of the weak points in our official view of writing and literature. By making readers admit that it is difficult to explain why certain works are especially worthy or that letters cannot really counteract the effects of separation, he opens up the prospect of rethinking. His goal is to leave readers «contaminados» (PR, p. 59) with the obsessive need to ponder how literature can justify itself.

This search for a new self-inquiry also appears in the gross contradictions in Macedonio's own literary behavior. As we have seen, the author is not consistent in classifying all existing literature as «bad.» Exceptions to this characterization are continually arising. In particular, Twain, Quevedo, Gómez de la Serna and Cervantes elude the category «bad» although their works are already in existence. Another patent contradiction is between the author's rejection of didactic literature and his own need to teach the new esthetic. This becomes acute when Macedonio must teach or even preach the unacceptibility of the instructive author. [8] The fact that Macedonio must violate his own principles to move our culture toward a less rigid literary model is kept in the foreground. Readers are to recognize the irregular, paradoxical character of everything connected with literature. Here one may say that Macedonio seeks to garble the messages he sends to his audience, deliberately filling them with self-contradictory or nonsensical statements. The imperfections of his esthetic doctrine can prove productive in disrupting the reader's too-perfect conceptualization of literature.

The demand for ceaseless self-evaluation places Macedonio as a paradigmatically twentieth-century thinker. Recent years have seen manifestations of self-doubt in nearly all areas of human endeavor. To cite the example of one discipline, sociology has turned its methods of inquiry back upon itself, analyzing the premises and practices of sociological workers themselves. [9]

In his overview of the metasociological phenomenon, Frederick B. Lindstrom describes the reaction of certain sociologists to the profession's suddenly introspective mood: «Incestuous is the word some sociologists apply to the study of sociology by sociologists. Others find in such studies an embarassing similarity to an infant concentrating on its own internal workings. An unworthy thought is that no one other than a sociologist is really that interested in the sociology establishment, however fascinating its substantive findings often are to the wider public.»[10] Lindstrom himself expresses some concern lest the current focus on metasociology cause sociologists to lose sight of the larger societal panorama. So long as it is contextualized within the total inquiry into the nature of social phenomena, though, he sees self-study as a potentially productive sociological activity.[11]

The investigation of one's own workings has also been a salient feature of both literary creation and analysis in our time. The importance and necessity of such questioning is the theme of Frederic Jameson's 1971 essay, «Metacommentary.» In remarks whose impact on critics has been undeniable, Jameson points out that literature always contains a component of self-justification. Every literary writing implies why it ought to have been written at all. Recent literature has placed the commentary in a more visible position, making metaliterary concerns a predominant literary theme. Jameson recommends that criticism follow the model of literature in holding its own mechanisms subject to review. In his analysis, structural studies have limited their methodological validity by exempting their own investigative practices from self-justification:

> The starting point for any genuinely profitable discussion of interpretation therefore must be not the nature of interpretation, but the need for it in the first place. What initially needs explanation is, in other words, not how we go about interpreting a text properly, but rather why we should even have to do so. All thinking about interpretation must sink itself in the strangeness, the unnaturalness, of the hermeneutic situation; or to put it another way, every individual interpretation must include an interpretation of its own existence, must show its own credentials and justify itself; every commentary must be at the same time a metacommentary as well.[12]

Jameson urges structuralist literary critics not to cling to their theoretical models as the only possible expression of unalterable truths. Much more fruitful is to make theoretical premises historical, i.e., to view them as the product of a particular moment in the development of literary criticism. The critic should be aware that his model may grow obsolete. This consciousness implies a readiness to alter or discard part or all of the model as the needs of criticism change. Such willingness is part of the Macedonian innovation. The *Museo,* a pattern for the making of a «good» novel, officially allows future readers to modify or eliminate any part of the pattern incompatible with their reading needs (MNE, p. 265). Macedonio recognizes that future generations wil have a literary consciousness unlike our own (PR, p. 138) and will change literature accordingly.

Leaving the premises of one's work open to revision and the need for self-justification appear all through recent art and scholarship. Commenting on the criticism of Jitrik, David William Foster says:

> In it, Jitrik examines the changes in the *escritura* of the contemporary Latin-American narrative as the result of the metaliterary dictum involving self-conscious and self-justifying literature; it is a concern which, on the level of the structure of the literary work, fits in with the sort of critical imperative enunciated in his prologue with respect to the nature of literary criticism: *autocuestionamiento* is, in short, the byword of modern culture, as it and the scholarship that it generates measure themselves against the total human and social content of which it is a functioning part. [13]

Macedonio's flight from fixed principles and finished works reveal his intense participation in the twentieth-century movement to call all human endeavors into doubt and leave them permanently in such a situation.

NOTES

1. Derrida, *L'Ecriture et la différence,* p. 427.

2. Critics choosing to focus on Sarduy's reflection of social realities have included Ivan Schulman in his «*La situación* (obra de Lisandro Otero) y *Gestos:* dos visiones de la experiencia histórica cubana,» *Nueva narrativa hispanoamericana* 4 (1974), 345-72, and Donald R. Johndrow, «'Total' reality in Severo Sarduy's Search for *lo cubano*,» *Romance Notes,* 13 (1972), 445-52.

3. Iris Josefina Ludmer, *Cien años de soledad: una interpretación* (Buenos Aires: Tiempo Contemporáneo, 1972).

4. Ariel Dorfman, in particular, insists on the efficacy of so-called «magical realism» to transmit Third World realities. His best-known statement of this position is his *Imaginación y violencia en América* (Santiago de Chile: Editorial Universitaria, 1970). Dorfman's commentary on García Márquez, «La muerte como acto imaginativo en *Cien años de soledad,*» pp. 138-80 in the above-cited volume repeats Ludmer's idea that the «distortion» of the *nueva narrativa* may more accurately be seen as a mythically true representation.

5. Jitrik comments on the difference between Macedonio and the *nueva narrativa* obliquely in his essay «Bipolaridad en la historia de la literatura argentina,» included in his *Ensayos y estudios de literatura argentina* (Buenos Aires: Galerna, 1970), p. 239. The critic observes that Macedonio's obsessive concern with abstraction and mental activity makes his work susceptible to possible co-optation, i.e., transformation into «offical» literature.

6. García makes this observation in his interview with Marechal, p. 73 in above-cited compilation.

7. Jitrik, «La 'novela futura' de Macedonio Fernández,» p. 164.

8. For notably «preachy» Macedonian writings, see the *Museo de la novela de la Eterna,* p. 23-24, 31-34, 68-70; for his censure of didacticism in literature, see Fernández Moreno, pp. 16-17.

9. Typical examples of «metasociological» writings include: *Professing Sociology* (1968) by Irving Louis Horowitz, *Sociology* (1969) by Neil J. Smelser and James A. Davis, *Approaching Sociology; A Critical Introduction* (1970) by Margaret A. Coulson and David S. Riddle, *A Sociology of Sociology* (1970) by Robert W. Friedrichs, *The Coming Crisis of Western Sociology* by Alvin W. Gouldner (1970) and *The Romance of a Profession: A Case History in the Sociology of Sociology* (1976) by Don Martingale.

10. Frederick B. Lindstrom, «Sociology Today, Yesterday and Tomorrow,» *Rocky Mountain Social Science Journal,* 9, 1 (1972), 143.

11. Lindstrom, pp. 143-47.

12. Frederic Jameson, «Metacommentary,» *PMLA,* 86 (1971), 10.

13. Foster, «Not the Same Old Wine in New Bottles,» *Chasqui,* 5, 2 (1976), 72.

SELECTED BIBLIOGRAPHY

The recent resurgence of interest in Macedonio Fernández has greatly altered the character of the bibliography on the singular innovator. When Horacio J. Becco compiled his 1960 complete bibliography (see below), the Macedonian *oeuvre* was dispersed in long-out-of-print books and defunct vanguardistic magazines. With relatively few exceptions, critical discussion had not progressed beyond journalistic notes and personal reminiscences.

The accessibility of Macedonian texts increased dramatically with Centro Editor de América Latina's publication of *Papeles de recienvenido* (1966) and *Museo de la novela de la Eterna* (1967). Ediciones Corregidor subsequently became interested in Macedonio's work and in 1974, the centennial of his birth, began producing a series of *Obras completas.*

The existence of this large, readily accessible corpus in book form obviates the need to relist the original periodical sources, although we have listed all first editions of books. We have not listed recent miscellaneous Macedoniana such as the personal letters *Crisis* (Buenos Aires) printed in its May-June (pp. 10-15) and July (pp. 59-63) 1976 issues.

The standing criticism on Macedonio now includes a good number of monographic studies and journal articles. Its improved status justifies our omission of the more ephemeral types of commentary. Most of the studies listed represent inquiries into the stylistic, structural, thematic or literary-historical aspects of Macedonio's innovation. We have also included a few «testimonies» by the author's literary acquaintances. These accounts provide an idea of the literary inventions Macedonio only conceptualized, never committing them to paper.

Readers looking for a more exhaustive, if less up-to-date, bibliography should consult Becco's 1960 listing, to which we are indebted.

Bibliography

1. Bibliographies of Macedonio Fernández

Becco, Horacio Jorge. «Bibliografía de Macedonio Fernández.» In Noé Jitrik, *La novela futura de Macedonio Fernández*, Caracas: Universidad Central de Venezuela, 1973, pp. 125-44.

«Bibliografía de Macedonio Fernández.» In César Fernández Moreno, *Introducción a Macedonio Fernández*. Buenos Aires: Editorial Talía, 1960, pp. 39-46.

2. Books by Macedonio Fernández

No toda es vigilia la de los ojos abiertos (Arreglo de papeles que dejó un personaje de novela creado por el arte, Deunamor el No Existente Caballero, el estudioso de su esperanza.) Buenos Aires: Manuel Gleizer, 1928.

Papeles de recienvenido. Buenos Aires: Editorial Proa, 1929.

Una novela que comienza. Santiago de Chile: Editorial Ercilla, 1941.

Muerte es beldad. La Plata, Argentina: Ediciones de M.F., 1942.

Papeles de recienvenido. Continuación de la nada. Buenos Aires: Editorial Losada, 1944.

Poemas. Mexico City: Editorial Guaranía, 1953.

Macedonio Fernández. Borges, Jorge Luis, ed. Buenos Aires: Ediciones Culturales Argentinas, Colección Antologías, 1961.

Papeles de recienvenido, poemas, relatos, cuentos, miscelánea. Buenos Aires: Centro Editor de América Latina, 1966.

Museo de la novela de la Eterna. Buenos Aires: Centro Editor, 1967.

No toda es vigilia la de los ojos abiertos (Arreglo de papeles que dejó un personaje de novela creado por el arte, Deunamor el No Existente Caballero, el estudioso de su esperanza.). Buenos Aires: Centro Editor, 1967.

Papeles de recienvenido. La Habana, Cuba: Casa de las Americas, 1969.

Cuadernos de todo y nada. Buenos Aires: Ediciones Corregidor, 1972.

Teorías. Buenos Aires: Corregidor, 1974 (t. III of his *Obras completas)*.

Adriana Buenos Aires. Ultima novela mala. Buenos Aires: Corregidor, 1974, (t. V of *Obras completas)*.

Museo de la novela de la Eterna. Buenos Aires: Corregidor, 1974 (t. VI of *Obras completas*).

Manera de una psique sin cuerpo (antología). Tomás Guido Lavalle, ed. Barcelona: Tusqueta Editor, 1975.

Epistolario. Alicia Borinsky, ed. Buenos Aires: Corregidor, 1976. (t. VI of *Obras completas*).

Macedonio (anthology), Jo Anne Engelbert, ed. New York: Center for Inter-American Relations (forthcoming).

3. Books on Macedonio Fernández

Borinsky, Alicia. *Humorística, novelística y obra abierta en Macedonio Fernández*. Unpublished doctoral dissertation, University of Pittsburgh, 1971. Available through University Microfilms, Ann Arbor, Michigan.

——————. *Macedonio y sus otros*. Buenos Aires: Corregidor, forthcoming.

Engelbert, Jo Anne. *Macedonio Fernández and the Spanish American New Novel*. New York: New York University/ Center for Inter-American Relations. 1977.

Fernández Moreno, César. *Introducción a Macedonio Fernández*. Buenos Aires: Emecé, 1956. Rev. ed., Editorial Talía, 1960.

Flammersfeld, Waltraut. *Macedonio Fernández (1874-1952): Reflexion und Negation als Bestimmungen der Modernität*. Frankfurt: Peter Lang, 1976.

Foix, Juan Carlos. *Macedonio Fernández*. Buenos Aires: Editorial Bonum, 1974.

García, Germán Leopoldo, ed. *Jorge Luis Borges, Arturo Jauretche, et. al hablan de Macedonio Fernández* (book of interviews). Buenos Aires: Carlos Pérez, 1969.

——————. *Macedonio Fernández: la escritura en objeto*. Buenos Aires: Siglo Veintiuno, 1975.

Jitrik, Noé. *La novela futura de Macedonio Fernández*. Caracas: Universidad Central de Venezuela, 1973. This volume contains Jitrik's below-cited article and supplementary documents.

Obieta, Adolfo de. *Papeles de Macedonio Fernández*. Buenos

Aires: Editorial Universitaria de Buenos Aires, 1964.
Tripoli, Vicente. *Macedonio Fernández, esbozo de una inteligencia.* Buenos Aires: Editorial Colombo, 1964.

4. Critical Articles and Discussion in Books.

Barrenechea, Ana María. «Macedonio Fernández y su humorismo de la nada.» *Buenos Aires Literaria,* No. 9 (1953). 25-38. Also as «La creación de la nada en el humorismo de Macedonio Fernández». In *La literatura fantástica en Argentina* (with Emma S. Speratti Pinero). Mexico City: Editorial Imprenta Universitaria, 1957. Pp. 37-53. Also as «Macedonio Fernández y su humorismo de la nada.» In Jorge Lafforgue, ed., *Nueva novela latinoamericana,* 2. Buenos Aires: Paidós, 1972. Pp. 71-88.
Biagini, Hugo E. «Macedonio Fernández, pensador político.» *Hispamérica,* No. 21 (1978). 11-20.
Borges, Jorge Luis. «Macedonio Fernández.» *Sur* (Buenos Aires), No. 209-10 (1952). 145-47.
_____. Preface to his anthology *Macedonio Fernández.* Buenos Aires: Ediciones Culturales Argentinas, 1961. Pp. 7-22. Also in *Review of the Center for Inter-American Relations,* No. 21-22 (1977). 129-33. As «A Prologue,» trans. Gregory Kolovakos.
Borinsky, Alicia. «Correspondencia de Macedonio Fernández a Gómez de la Serna.» *Revista Iberoamericana,* No. 36 (1970). 101-23.
_____. «Macedonio: su proyecto novelístico,» *Hispamérica,* 1, 1 (1972) 31-48.
_____. «Macedonio y el humor de Julio Cortázar,» *Revista Iberoamericana,* Nos. 84-85 (1973). 521-35.
Canal Feijóo, Bernardo. «Teoría de Macedonio Fernández.» *Revista Davar* (Buenos Aires), No. 1 (1945). 61-67.
Casasbellas, Ramiro de. «Lugones y Macedonio Fernández: la fuerza y el sueño.» In Casasbellas et al., *Ocho escritores por ocho periodistas* Buenos Aires: Timerman Editores, 1976. Pp. 100-108.
Cuneo, Dardo. *El romanticismo político (Lugones, Payró, Ingenieros, Macedonio Fernández, Ugarte, Gerchunoff).* Buenos Aires: Ediciones Transición, 1955. Pp. 85-92.

Echavarren, Roberto. «La estética de Macedonio Fernández.» *Revista Iberoamericana,* Nos. 106-107 (1979), 31-48.

Engelbert, Jo Anne. «Chronology.» *Review of the Center for Inter-American Relations,* No. 22 (1977). 119-22.

García, Germán L. «Desvivirse de Macedonio Fernández.» In his *Jorge Luis Borges, Arturo Jauretche, et. al hablan de Macedonio Fernández.* Buenos Aires: Carlos Pérez, 1969. Pp. 103-27.

Ghiano, Juan Carlos. «Los poemas de Macedonio Fernández.» *Sur,* No. 231 (1954). 109-114.

_____. «Poesía filosófica: Macedonio Fernández.» In his *Poesía argentina del siglo XX.* Mexico City: Fondo de Cultura Económica, 1957. Pp. 98-101.

Gómez de la Serna, Ramón. «Silueta de Macedonio Fernández.» *Sur,* No. 28 (1937). 75-83.

_____. «Macedonio Fernández.» In his *Retratos contemporáneos.* Buenos Aires: Editorial Losada, 1944. Pp. 153-74.

_____. Preface to Fernández, *Papeles de recienvenido. Continuación de la nada.* Buenos Aires: Editorial Losada, 1944. Pp. 7-46.

Jitrik, Noé. «La 'novela futura' de Macedonio Fernández.» In his *El fuego de la especie.* Buenos Aires: Siglo Veintiuno, 1971, Pp. 151-88. Also in Lafforgue. *Nueva novela latinoamericana.* Pp. 30-70. Also in *Review of the Center for Inter-American Relations,* No. 21-22 (1977), 137-148, as «The Future Novel.» Trans. William Ciamurro. A selection appears as «Retrato discontinuo de Macedonio Fernández.» *Ideas, letras, ideas en la crisis* (Buenos Aires. No. 3 (1973). 44-49.

_____. Discussion of Fernández in *El no existente caballero: la idea de personaje y su evolución en la narrativa latinoamericana.* Buenos Aires: Megápolis, 1975. Pp. 67-77.

Jurado, Alicia. «Aproximación a Macedonio Fernández.» *Ficción* (Buenos Aires), No. 7 (1957). 65-78.

Kamenszain, Tamara. «El texto que se sabe.» *Hispamérica,* 3, 7 (1974). 57-59.

Lafforgue, Jorge. «La narrative argentina actual.» In his *Nueva novela latinoamericana.* Pp. 16-18.

Lindstrom, Naomi. «Macedonio Fernández: An Argentine Author of the Unwritten.» *Latin American Digest,* 11, 4-12, 1 (1977-78). 1-3.

_____. «Who is Macedonio Fernández?» *Affinities,* Forthcoming.

_____. «La reinvención del discurso metafísico en Macedonio Fernández,» *Cathedra,* forthcoming.

_____. «Macedonio Fernández and Jacques Derrida: Co-Visionaries.» *Review of the Center for Inter-American Relations,* No. 21-22 (1977). 149-54.

_____. «Macedonio Fernández: Strategies Against Readerly Sloth.» *Latin American Literary Review,* 4, 11 (1977). 81-88.

_____. Discussion in *Literary Expressionism in Argentina: The Presentation of Incoherence.* Tempe: Center for Latin American Studies, 1977. Pp. 52-60, 83-88.

Martini Real, Juan Carlos. «El legado de Macedonio.» *Macedonio* (Buenos Aires), No. 11 (1971). 3-9.

Morales, Miguel Angel. «Macedonio Fernández: la alquimia de la metafísica,» *Revista de la Universidad de México,* 31, 6 (1977). 29-33.

Murchison, John. «The Visible Work of Macedonio Fernández.» *Books Abroad,* 45, 3 (1971). 427-34. Also in Lowell Dunham and Ivar Ivask, eds., *The Cardinal Points of Borges.* Norman, Oklahoma: University of Oklahoma Press, 1971, Pp. 55-62.

Obieta, Adolfo de. «Advertencia.» Preface to «Inéditos de Macedonio Fernández.» *Hispamérica,* 1, 1 (1972). 49-51.

_____. «My Father, Macedonio Fernández.» *Review of the Center for Inter-American Relations,* No. 21-22 (1977). 126-28.

Pagés Larraya, Antonio. «Macedonio Fernández: un payador.» *Buenos Aires Literaria,* No. 9 (1953). 39-50.

Rodríguez Monegal, Emir. «Macedonio Fernández, Borges y el ultraísmo.» *Número* (Montevideo), No. 19 (1952). 171-83.

Sálvador, Nélida. «Macedonio Fernández y su poemática del pensar.» *Comentario,* 14, 56 (1967), 9-18.

_____. «La negación de la realidad en los cuentos de Macedonio Fernández.» *Comentario,* 14, 56 (1967), 9-18.

_____. «Macedonio Fernández.» In Pedro Orgambide and Roberto Yahni, eds., *Enciclopedia de la literatura argentina.* Buenos Aires: Sudamericana, 1970. Pp. 229-34.

Scalabrini Ortiz, Raúl. «Macedonio.» In his *El hombre que está solo y espera.* Buenos Aires: Editorial Plus Ultra, 1964, P. 125.

_____. «Macedonio, nuestro primer metafísico.» *Nosotros*

(Buenos Aires), 23, 228 (1928). 235-40.
Scrimaglio, Marta. *Literatura argentina de vanguardia* (1920-1930). Buenos Aires: Editorial Biblioteca, 1974. Pp. 117-24, 126-27.

CHRONOLOGY

1874	Macedonio Fernández is born in Buenos Aires.
1896	Publishes three philosophical articles in *El Tiempo* (Carlos Vega Belgrano, ed.)
1897	Despite erratic habits of study, Macedonio obtains a doctor of jurisprudence degree from the Universidad de Buenos Aires. Macedonio helps found a short-lived utopian commune in Paraguay. He propounds an idealistic mixture of socialistic and anarchistic principles.
1901	Marriage to Elena de Obieta.
1901-20	Macedonio only sporadically practices the legal profession. He formulates his ideas on metaphysics and poetics through reading, discussion and correspondences with William James and Ramón Gómez de la Serna.
1920	Death of Elena de Obieta. Macedonio disperses his immediate family and begins to live eccentrically in boarding-houses.
1921	Return of young Jorge Luis Borges to Buenos Aires. Borges, seeking to promote vanguardistic literary experimentation, involves the retiring Macedonio in literary life. The older man becomes a hero to the group of literary radicals gathered around Borges.
1922	Borges makes Macedonio co-founder of the vanguard magazine *Proa*.
1923-29	Macedonio is active in many of the vanguard group's events. He attends numerous banquets and discussions and receives the young writers' visits. However, his literary program is not well understood by the vanguardists in general. The older man's writings appear in the young people's magazines and newspapers, most notably in *Martín Fierro*.

1928   At the insistence of Raúl Scalabrini Ortiz, Oliverio
         Girondo and Leopoldo Marechal, Macedonio allows
         a collection of his metaphysical reflections to be
         published as *No toda es vigilia la de los ojos abiertos.*

1929   A miscellany of Macedonio's writings appears under
         the title *Papeles de recienvenido.*

1930   Macedonio drifts away from the vanguard group,
         which by now has become somewhat dispersed.

1941   Alberto Hidalgo edits and publishes Macedonio's
         Una novela que comienza in Santiago de Chile with
         Ercilla publishing house.

1942   Marcos Fingerit produces an edition of *Muerte es
         beldad,* poems by Macedonio.

1943   Macedonio and his sons found a small review,
         Papeles de Buenos Aires.

MACEDONIO FERNANDEZ